11,000 EMPLOYEES. 233 OFFICES. 75 COUNTRIES. 2.9 BILLION E-MAILS. 530 MILLION CELLPHONE CALLS. 838 MILLION TEXTS. 945 MILLION INSTANT MESSAGES. 12 MILLION TWEETS. 3 MILLION GALLONS OF COFFEE. 11 MILLION CONFERENCE CALLS. 8 MILLION SHOTS OF ESPRESSO. 4 MILLION CHAI LATTES. 7 MILLION GLAZED DONUTS. 5 MILLION PEPPERONI PIZZAS. 3 MILLION CLIENT PRESENTATIONS. OVER 2 MILLION LATE-NIGHT DINNER DELIVERIES. GAZILLIONS OF DOODLES. 10 YEARS OF CREATIVE BUSINESS IDEAS.

★ EURO RSCG WORLDWIDE

THE CREATIVE BUSINESS IDEABOOK

A Smallwood & Stewart Book

CONTENTS

FROM WAR ROOM TO BOARDROOM: THE ELEVATION OF CREATIVITY

Great ideas win. They sink their claws into slippery attention spans and don't let go. They erupt and disrupt. They change how people think and influence what people do. And, at a time when there are more players, more products, and less reach than ever before, they have enormous power to build businesses and brands.

Our industry has seen all sorts of changes in the past decade but none more framework-shaking than the movement of creativity beyond agency war rooms and into corporate boardrooms. Where it once was an adjunct component of business, now creativity is recognized as a critical differentiator and driver of growth. Come up with a brilliant idea, figure out how to engage people in it, and that idea will have the power to carry your message around the globe.

In 2000, our agency network came up with a term to describe the sort of ideas that are so powerful they can transform businesses, create entirely new categories, and alter consumer perceptions. We call them Creative Business Ideas® and they are something we aspire to conceive and put to work on behalf of every client on our roster every day.

It's a fascinating time to be in the communications business. All too often, the most awarded work within our industry has not been the most effective. Advertisements were lauded as brilliant when they were visually stunning and creatively exciting. Whether they sold products and helped to build the client's business was beside the point. Growing the business was the job of the workhorse ads, those repetitive jingles and omnipresent commercials that trumpeted the same product claims ad nauseam until people started buying the concept—and the product.

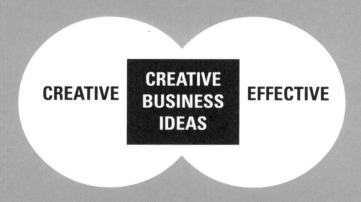

Creative Business Ideas sit at
the intersection of creativity and effectiveness.

Now rote repetition is no longer enough to capture an audience, much less build customer loyalty. Increased competition, saturated markets, and sliced-and-diced audiences mean every business must fight every second to be heard. This new playing field demands constant engagement and the building of real and lasting connections between consumer and brand. The best way to build those connections is to bring to life an idea so powerful it is capable of persuading consumers to actively pursue a relationship with the brand, not vice versa.

Think about how many of today's leading businesses and brands were built on the backs of brilliant ideas. Over the past couple of decades, companies have come out of nowhere to dominate or even create categories. eBay got millions of people involved in buying and selling at the world's biggest garage sale. Google figured out how to put virtually all the world's information in one place. Apple invested technology with emotional appeal by merging it with design.

Creativity and commerce may once have been, at best, tolerant bedfellows, but they are now full partners. The most successful businesses will be those that most effectively harness the power of ingenuity and innovation.

The future is a simple game: Whoever has the best idea will win. By sharing some of our most powerful—and effective—ideas within this book, it is our hope that we will raise the bar on creative engagement even further.

BIRTH OF THE
CREATIVE BUSINESS IDEA

ADVERTISING IS DEAD. Or so pronounced an assortment of soothsayers in 1999. And they had a point: The old way of advertising was dead, or at least in its last throes. The notion of families—entire nations even—gathered in front of a television set and passively viewing a standard lineup of programs and commercials had gone the way of the Betamax. Consumer audiences had been splintered by burgeoning channels of communication and a rapid increase in content. Enemies of advertising were spotted everywhere: in the remote controls that allowed audiences to surf through hundreds of cable and satellite TV channels, in the dastardly invention of the digital video recorder (TiVo and ReplayTV launched that year), in the rapid adoption of the Internet (more than four in ten U.S. households were already online).

What was an advertiser to do? That was the question Bob Schmetterer, then-chairman and CEO of Euro RSCG Worldwide, put to participants at the International Advertising Festival in Cannes in 1999. His answer: Stop thinking that advertising is about ads. It isn't. It is about brilliantly integrated creative ideas. At the time, these ideas didn't have a name within the agency network. But we knew them when we saw them. And we also knew, beyond any doubt, that they represented the future of Euro RSCG and the communications industry. In 2000, an agency team set about formalizing our approach to these ideas, starting with a name: **The Creative Business Idea.** We introduced our new platform to the industry, again at Cannes.

What exactly is a Creative Business Idea—or CBI? From the outset, we wanted to distinguish between CBIs and plain old good ideas. Our decision in 2000 to make the Volvo S60 the first car to be launched exclusively online was a good idea—a great idea even, judging by all the media coverage—but it did not fundamentally change the business or the brand. And that, we realized, is precisely what a CBI does. The team charged with developing the CBI tool came up with this definition:

A Creative Business Idea...
Is Transformational
Changes Business Strategy
Drives Profitable Growth

That last aspect cannot be overstated, for the purpose of CBIs is not to win awards or to give the agency bragging rights but to build our clients' businesses and brands. These are ideas that transcend media, adaptable to both traditional and emerging formats. They are ideas that very often don't change simply how consumers view a company but how a company views itself, removing burdensome constraints and offering the business new spaces in which to explore and grow.

Since 2000, Creative Business Ideas have been the mantra, mission, and mark of distinction of Euro RSCG. They are the obsession of the more than 11,000 professionals in our 233 offices in 75 countries and the promise we make to clients across categories and around the globe. Our disciplined approach to creative thinking has propelled our growth into the largest agency in the world by number of global accounts. It infuses our work in advertising, digital, social media, marketing services, healthcare, public relations, and corporate communications. And it drives our efforts to rethink what is possible for our agency, our industry, and our client brands.

With this book, we celebrate our first decade of CBIs, spotlighting select cases in a broad array of industries and in markets as disparate as the United States, United Arab Emirates, France, and India. Each case study, each business success, each brand transformation is centered on one simple component: a core idea so powerful, so compelling it creates a better future for the business or brand.

Our focus as an agency is on getting our clients to the future first. We do this by knowing everything we can about our client brands, their categories, and their consumers, and then using that knowledge and insight to consistently deliver brilliant Creative Business Ideas that drive growth. If our ideas succeed, our clients succeed—and so we succeed. It's as simple as that.

Our Process {

Creative Business Ideas are fueled by inspiration. But they are also the product of focused cross-examination and research. Before we convince a client to invest time and money in an idea, we need to be certain of the payoff. And that means we have to combine creativity and discipline, developing a structured approach to the creation and implementation of our ideas.

In the initial stage of our process, we gather information and insights in order to get as smart as possible about the brand in question, its category, and its consumers. We do this with the assistance of three proprietary tools—each one future focused and predictive in nature:

• **Prosumers:** Since 2002, Euro RSCG has invested some $6 million in an ongoing study of a group of leading-edge consumers we call "Prosumers." These highly influential men and women are using new communications channels and access to information to shift the balance of power away from companies and toward themselves. In every category and locale, these are the people who are making and breaking markets. (See chapter 5 for more detail.)

• **Brand Momentum:** With this tool we measure a brand's position in the marketplace—paying attention to trust (experience) and dynamism (potential)—and the rate at which it is gaining or losing ground vis-à-vis its competitors.

• **Decipher:** Each brand category has its own language composed of words, sights, and sounds that speak to consumers. Our Decipher tool uncovers the emergent communication codes within any category in order that we may spot opportunities and explore fresh ways of thinking.

Once our intelligence is in place, we examine the intersections between each component (consumers, brand, category) to identify areas in which we can increase brand relevance and magnify the brand's advantage over competitors. We then work with the client to generate a number of forward-thinking strategic ideas that play into the intersections identified. And, finally, we agree on, articulate, and flesh out the single most powerful idea: the Creative Business Idea.

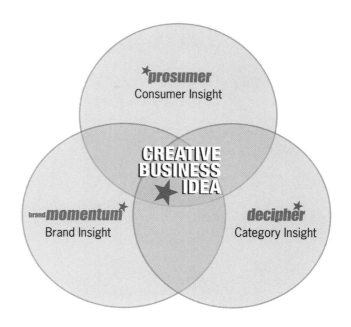

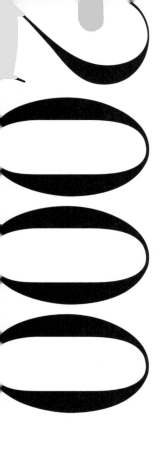

In 2000, Euro RSCG Worldwide launched the Creative Business Idea Awards, an agencywide contest to foster—and reward—exemplary high-level creative thinking. Each year, the jury is composed of top strategic, media, and creative thinkers both from within and beyond the agency network. Outside jurors have included Andrew Jaffe, executive director of the Clio Awards; Bill Taylor, co-founder of *Fast Company* magazine; Professor Douglas Holt of the Harvard Business School; and Tom Kelley, general manager of IDEO. The contest is open to all Euro RSCG agencies, and the winning teams walk away with substantial cash prizes. Here we honor our first decade of recipients:

2000
Gold: Euro RSCG Sydney, Hutchison Telecom Australia, "Orange One"
Silver: Euro RSCG New York, Volvo Cars, "Revolvolution"
Bronze: Euro RSCG Bikker and Euro RSCG 4D Amsterdam, Nokia, "Nokia Game"

2001
Gold: Euro RSCG Buenos Aires, Billiken, "Billiken Club"
Silver: BETC Euro RSCG, RATP, "Mobility Provider"
Bronze: Euro RSCG Sweden, The Ministry of Color, "Room Service"

2002
Gold: BETC Euro RSCG, Hollywood Chewing Gum, "Changing Hollywood"
Silver: Euro RSCG 4D Brazil, Intel, "Intel Next Generation Center"
Bronze: Euro RSCG C&O, Airbus, "A380 Launch"

2003
Gold: BETC Euro RSCG, Evian, "Waterboy"
Silver: BETC Euro RSCG, INPES, "Anti-Smoking Campaign"
Bronze: Euro RSCG New York, Polaroid, "Polaroid Ambush"

2004
Gold: Euro RSCG 4D France and BETC Euro RSCG, Carrefour, "Carte Carrefour"
Silver: Euro RSCG Guangzhou, China Mobile, "Live in the News"
Bronze: Fuel Europe, Volvo Cars, "The Mystery of Dalarö"

CREATIVE BUSINESS IDEA  Awards

2005

Gold (Global): Euro RSCG New York, Jaguar, "Gorgeous"
Gold (Local): Euro RSCG Zürich, Migros, "M-Budget Mobile"

Silver (Global): BETC Euro RSCG, Louis Vuitton, "Travel"
Silver (Local): Euro RSCG India, Mortein (Reckitt Benckiser), "Modern-Day Ramayana"

2006

Gold: Euro RSCG New York, Charles Schwab, "Talk to Chuck"
Silver: Euro RSCG India, The All India Gems & Jewellery Trade Federation, "Lucky Lakshmi"
Bronze: BETC Euro RSCG, Air France, "Making the Sky the Best Place on Earth"

2007

Gold: Euro RSCG New York, Dos Equis, "The Most Interesting Man in the World"
Silver: Euro RSCG India, "The Predictameter"
Bronze: BETC Euro RSCG, eBay, "You Are eBay"

2008

Gold: EHS 4D, DECC, "The Carbon Calculator"
Silver: BETC Euro RSCG, McDonald's, "Come As You Are"
Bronze: Euro RSCG New York, *The Atlantic*, "Think. Again."

2009

Gold: BETC Euro RSCG, Evian, "Roller Babies"
Silver: BETC Euro RSCG, Canal+, "The Power of Great Stories"
Bronze: Euro RSCG London/THE:HOURS/Euro RSCG Worldwide/Euro RSCG Prague,
  Global Humanitarian Forum, "TckTckTck"

2010

Gold: Euro RSCG Worldwide, "One Young World"
Silver: Euro RSCG London, Dulux, "Let's Color"
Bronze: BETC Euro RSCG, 13ème Rue, "Unleash the Criminal Mind in You"

2010

"Fundamentally, it really is a brilliant time to be in our business. Today brands are more important because, with more and more competition and more and more clutter, a powerful brand that cuts through is critical. Creativity and ideas are much more important than in the old days when people were stuck in front of their TVs and we could put whatever nonsense on and they had to watch it. Now, if you don't engage people they won't pay attention."

—David Jones, Global CEO, Havas and
  Euro RSCG Worldwide

"WE CAN NO LONGER REACH AND INFLUENCE CONSUMERS IN THE WAY WE DID OVER THE LAST HUNDRED YEARS. COMMUNICATION HAS TO BRING MORE RELEVANCE TO PEOPLE'S LIVES."

—Andreas Geyr, CEO, Euro RSCG Europe

"The advent of the web and digital communication in general has posed both a threat to and an opportunity for our industry. We are fighting for our relevance as consumers become ever more conscious of their choices and have access to 'search engines' in every quadrant of their lives. That all-important 'announcement' capacity the advertising industry used to represent is being diluted every day, with every laptop, mobile phone, tablet sold across the world." —Ricardo Monteiro, CEO, Euro RSCG Ibero-America

UNLEASHING HUMAN VIRUSES

BUZZ has been around far longer than the word has been used to describe it. Centuries ago, opera singers would hire people to shout "Bravo" at the end of arias to get the applause rolling, and in the 1800s P.T. Barnum created such a frenzy around his traveling circus that tales of the performance would start circulating weeks before its arrival and continue to spread after the performers had packed up and left town.

There's a new circus these days, and it's *always* in town. Instead of just three rings, the modern equivalent runs on countless stages playing out 24/7/365 across the Internet—and social media has turned those rings into ever-reverberating circles of influence through which we're all players, to a lesser or greater degree, in the art of buzz. When you "like" someone, or something, on Facebook, when you Digg or retweet a post or share a video on YouTube, you are serving as a buzz accelerant—as a buzz marketer, even—regardless of whether that is truly your intent.

The viral nature of the Internet is such that anything that captures the public's imagination can wend its way around the world in a matter of days, if not hours. When Scottish singer Susan Boyle made her brilliant debut on *Britain's Got Talent*, her audition was seen by some 10.3 million TV viewers in the U.K. Within little more than a week, it had been viewed by *ten times* that many people on YouTube—and from all around the world. Within a year, the video had been watched 360 million times. "It was the kind of global celebrity it took the Beatles years to achieve, Madonna, perhaps, a decade or more," wrote journalist Carole Cadwalladr in *The Observer*. "It's a kind of fame that hasn't happened to anyone ever before. Not on this scale. In this way. This was something of a whole new order: a new kind of fame created by new forms of communication, a throwaway item made for TV that travelled as far and wide as the web would take it, and Susan Boyle, a 47-year-old, unmarried woman from a former mining town in rural Scotland, was its first test case."

Such was her fame and popularity that Boyle's first CD became Amazon.com's all-time best-selling album in presales three months prior to release. It topped music charts around the world and enjoyed the largest sales debut in history for a female artist.

Any company would pay a hefty sum to obtain even a fraction of the public exposure that Boyle garnered literally overnight, and yet it cost her not a penny. For marketers, the lesson is clear: Get people sufficiently interested in your product or brand, and they will do the promotional work for you—and faster and more efficiently than you could possibly achieve on your own. This buzz principle even applies to the building of corporate brands. Think about eBay and Google and Starbucks, three hugely successful companies that have come to dominate entire categories, not through enormous advertising outlays but through plain old word of mouth. Loyal users of each of these brands took it upon themselves to tell others about their great experiences. And the companies grew beyond all expectations as a result.

This sort of organic customer evangelism doesn't mean companies don't have to make an effort to bolster and spread the positive buzz. Looking at the three giants just mentioned, we see that each one has been relentless about finding new ways to involve consumers in its brand. eBay's user base is intrinsically active—whether as buyers or sellers or both; Google famously invites its users to test its new products in beta form and submit feedback; and Starbucks engages its customers in a number of ways, including actively encouraging volunteerism through such programs as Make Your Mark and its partnership with HandsOn Network.

Making customers feel like part of a brand community gives them a sense of emotional investment in a brand and its future, and this in turn motivates people to talk it up to others and invite them to join in. Consider Craigslist, the seventh largest Internet company in the world when measured by English-language page views. Not only does it not advertise, it doesn't even have a logo. What it *does* have is a community of more than 60 million users in the United States alone, operating with a staff of just 30.

In this chapter, we look at a handful of companies—Polaroid, Volvo, Evian, Mortein, and Dos Equis—that have used viral marketing to grow their businesses, energize their brands, and capture new audiences. They represent a broad variety of industries and have used markedly different approaches to get people's tongues wagging and fingers clicking, from humor to intrigue and adventure, from pop culture to voyeurism, and yet they all have excelled by focusing on three fundamentals of buzz: breaking people away from their routines, giving them something to talk about, and making it easy to share. In the new environment fueled by social media, all it takes is one great idea to unleash the P.T. Barnum within us all.

POLAROID
"AMBUSH"

HOW CAN OLD MEDIA BECOME NEW MEDIA?

In 2003, Polaroid was a brand loved by many, used by few. The instant camera was a throwback to leisure suits and vinyl records, a bit of kitschy fun in a digital world. What chance did Polaroid's brand of "instant" photography stand against all the latest-in-tech players?

The digital age had redefined the word *instant*. In photography, it meant snapping a photo and viewing it immediately on an LCD screen, not waiting several minutes for a swatch of wet film to develop. Polaroid had its fans, but nothing seemed as "now" as digital. Still, the iconic brand was poised to unveil ZINK, a portable one-step printer. The company was still recovering from filing for bankruptcy protection—digital cameras and photo huts had been hard blows—when Euro RSCG New York won the business.

SHAKE IT

What Polaroid needed was to be blasted out of the past and into the Now. It needed to be part of pop culture. "The thought was that there are all these people who are cultural pacesetters who still love Polaroid," says Linda Lewi, then CMO of the client company. "We have to connect with them and become part of their cultural sphere." With help from Euro RSCG's buzz team, Polaroid cameras made it onto the tables at Cynthia Rowley's Fashion Week show in New York and to the Sundance Film Festival in Telluride, Colorado. These events touched highbrow artists and designers, but the mass market remained untapped.

What happened next was a combination of serendipity, marketing savvy, and hustle. Hip-hop duo Andre 3000 and Big Boi, performing under the name OutKast, released "Hey Ya!"—a single with a shoutout not to Burberry, Bentley, or Cristal, but to Polaroid. "Shake it like a Polaroid picture" may have been a throwaway refrain, but for Polaroid it was a brilliant opportunity. Following a handshake deal in a hotel lounge, OutKast accepted free cameras in exchange for making use of them during their appearance on *Saturday Night Live*. From there, the song rose to the number one spot on the Billboard Hot 100 chart, taking Polaroid's visibility along for the ride.

The cameras were choreographed into OutKast's performances at the *Vibe* and Grammy awards, with dancers taking photos and waving them around while Andre 3000 encouraged the audience to "Shake it." They did.

In return, Polaroid sponsored OutKast's lavish after-parties. "We made sure they had the top party in town," Lewi says. "It became a virtuous circle of publicity." Andre 3000 and Big Boi even got Punk'd after one of the parties by a Polaroid-waving

Ashton Kutcher. By the time the NBA held its All-Star Game, producers were calling Euro RSCG asking if their client would donate 1,000 cameras in exchange for free placement. Teens circling the arena became Polarazzi, snapping pictures of athletes as they took to the court.

"WE HAD NO ADVERTISING BUDGET, AND WE HAD TO MAKE POLAROID HOT."

—Marian Salzman, CEO, Euro RSCG Worldwide PR, North America

The "Ambush" campaign ultimately racked up the equivalent of an estimated $4 million in media placements and earned the brand celebrity cachet as photos emerged of the camera in the hands of the likes of P. Diddy, Nicole Richie, Nicky Hilton, Macy Gray, Naomi Campbell, and the "Fab Five" from the new hot show *Queer Eye for the Straight Guy*. Baby boomers suddenly "remembered" what Polaroid had always stood for—instant fun—and their kids were introduced to the newest generation of products, including the sticker-producing i-Zone. Among Grammy viewers, Polaroid posted a 58 percent gain in relevance. Traffic to Polaroid.com in January and February of 2004 alone topped all of 2003. Online orders rose 90 percent.

The Polaroid camera had earned its way back into the cultural lexicon. No longer a dusty relic, it had a hit song, a fresh new profile—even its own dance! While the tremendous jolt of buzz Euro RSCG produced gave the brand a second shot at life, ultimately the underlying technology proved unable to sustain the momentum. Don't count it out yet, though: In 2010, Lady Gaga became the latest hit maker aligned with the brand. Great news, since Polaroid is one brand none of us wants to shake.

SHAKE IT LIKE A POLAROID PICTURE

HIP-HOP DUO OUTKAST RELEASES "HEY YA!"—

A SINGLE WITH A SHOUTOUT TO POLAROID

THE POLAROID DANCE IS BORN

Shake It Li[...]

Casting agent D. Nice has th[...] diamonds in the rough.

Mally guys dream of being multiplatinum artists—the fame, the money, the women. Especially the women, but for m[...] las, the fantasy will for[...] remain out of reach. Well, D[...] ren Malone, 32, better know[...] as D. Nice, has found another way to live the dream. As the founder of Nice Looks Casting, he gets paid to recruit bubbly, beautiful women for music videos by artists like Clipse, Ja Rule, and Avant. And Mr. Nice doesn't discriminate; tall or petite, thick or thin, as long as she catches the c[...] she might make it [...] screen. Gl[...]a Vel[...] now!

Jin[...]

Stars s[...]

stars in town knew where to c[...] *In Touch* studio! Our picture-p[...] Park City, Utah for the Sundan[...] ned photographer Kevin Mazu[...] using a special Polaroid camera,[...] her picture. "White teeth, wh[...] ress, who plans to give it to her[...] lanning used her acting skills t[...] ied boarding, but I bruised my[...] addition to hanging with our[...] time watching football with bu[...] impressive camera is one of fiv[...] ds and is five feet high. E[...]h shot costs $100 in [...] e think they're worth eve[...]nt! Say cheese!

VIBE

FASHION WEEK

The fey fashi[...] [...]es it up on the "[...] "Entertainmen[...] [...]s hit with a plas[...] [...]rom a balcony [...]n his way to [...]e picture taken [...] a Polaroid cam[...] [...]wood bash.

Kelly, Os[...]

[...]ackstage [...] for the pla[...] the Polaroid cameras on [...]es, where guests re [...] unifo[...] [...]tarella[...]

[...]e Anderson, who was walking the show. [...]wley might not have be[...] ble to get away [...]th using her Polaroid o[...] he Ol[...]pus- [...]nsored runways, but D[...] [...]ved with [...]r vintage Polaroid came[...] hoping to catch a [...]v snaps to add to her customized album. "I [...]ually take them on mov[...] [...]ey're so [...]ontaneous." And Bergm[...] [...]o quipped, "I [...]nk her clothes are real[...] [...]came [...]ause C[...]e is a big fan.

[...]problems [...] placem[...] of the [...]ol[...]oid [...]mer[...] on the [...]bles, [...]ere guests [...]e served by uni[...] wait[...]sses hired fr[...] Citaren[...] [...]epre[...]ntatives of b[...] Ms. R[...] and [...]h on S[...] delay[...] the [...]how's sta[...] for 45 m[...] utes while renegotiating the removal [...] the offending [...]

POLAROID POPS UP AT CELEBRITY PARTIES, FASHION WEEK SHOWS, THE MTV MUSIC AWARDS, THE GRAMMYS, THE SUNDANCE FILM FESTIVAL

NEW YORK TIMES · **NEW YORK POST**

Shake It!

SUNDANCE

awards

GRAMMYS

SNL

NBA ALL-STARS

FERE at Sundance

[...]e corn[...] [...]cted Kasm[...] al[...] [...]e calls [...]n[...] [...]cently h[...] dre[...] m[...] [...]nto canvas in the 1960s). [...]ay, the basement-level club in th[...] [...]p[...]na television marks the rise [...] fa[...] Fe[...]N[...] cate[...]ng [...]he [...]es like [...]er Jacobs In[...]u[...] [...]hi[...] [...]y bo[...] [...]med hi[...] b[...] [...]h a wash o[...] [...]hilip S[...] H[...]man a[...] Alan Cumming[...] att[...]ed [...]eni[...] Magnol[...] akery [...]me o[...] [...]med photographer Kevin Maz[...] [...]its using a special Polaroid camera[...] [...] her picture. "White teeth, wl[...] a [...]ress, who plans to give it to her[...] [...]vn Manning used her acting skills t[...]

Are you a th[...]mometer or a th[...]o[...] Do you guide tren[...] do trends gu[...] you? Read on t[...] F[...]ans list of yays and[...]

In Out

Polaroid One

WEBSITE TRAFFIC: UP SIXFOLD

25 MILLION PEOPLE REACHED

ONLINE SALES: + 90%

FIVE ESSENTIAL BUZZ BOOSTERS

What We've Learned from Polaroid and Others

Marian Salzman, CEO,
Euro RSCG Worldwide PR,
North America

The beauty—and peril—of viral marketing is that there is no surefire way to predict where a campaign will go once the match has been put to the fuse. Some will sputter and die away with no more than a pitiful wheeze. Others will explode in unexpected and undesired ways. And a fortunate few will exceed all expectations, lighting up the far reaches of the Internet and launching a product or brand into the stratosphere.

There is no sure way to anticipate or control buzz, but our experiences with Polaroid and other clients have taught us there are some guidelines that will maximize your chances of launching a winner.

CRUNCH THE NUMBERS

When Euro RSCG's New York agency was pitching the Polaroid account, the client team provided data on sales and market share. We chose to go the extra mile and commission independent qualitative and quantitative research in four key markets: the United States, the United Kingdom, Germany, and Japan. What we discovered was that Polaroid enjoyed enormous name recognition and was widely loved (especially in the U.S.), but was no longer seen as relevant or "of the moment." In a process we call *trendscouting*, the agency team surveyed our 11,000 colleagues in 75 countries, asking them to share their perspectives on the brand, its place and potential in their local markets, and how we could most effectively position it as one that lives in the "now." The resultant insights gave us an edge with our potential client, enabling us to pretest some of our early suppositions and refine our proposition.

Regardless of client category, research is a vital component of Euro RSCG's creative process. Through the Knowledge Exchange—a global team of strategic thinkers and an online repository of information and insights—the agency supplements local market and client-specific research by regularly fielding studies on a range of issues, including such topics as the rise in "mindful spending," the millennial generation's use of social media, and consumers' new definitions of value. These studies feed the agency's strategic creativity around the world.

CONDUCT A POP-CULTURE AUDIT

Most great advertising either reflects or inspires pop culture. When working with a brand that is perceived as somehow outmoded, we typically conduct a multimedia audit to determine where the brand sits—and should sit—within the broader culture. In the case of Polaroid, our audit turned up promising brand mentions in teen magazines, suggesting a point of entry. And, of course, we were already scanning the music charts when OutKast's "Hey Ya!" hit the scene, allowing us to jump on it before the song

had made its way up the charts and fully into the public consciousness.

CHOOSE YOUR WORDS WISELY

"It's not what you say but how you say it": We learned how spot-on that expression is a few years back when three Euro RSCG executives were promoting their new book, *Buzz: Harness the Power of Influence and Create Demand*, along with our latest study, The Future of Men. Our agency strategists had been talking about changes in men's lifestyles and interests for years, including what we considered the "feminization" of a substantial number of straight men—guys who were visiting spas for facials, spending lots of time shopping for clothes, and getting more involved in home decor and cooking. It made for some productive client meetings, but our research attracted little media interest. That all changed in 2003, when we dropped the "M" bomb: *metrosexual*. Applied to our research, that one little word created a media explosion. We didn't even invent the term, but we redefined it and pushed it into everyday use. The reaction was swift and explosive: From the U.S. and U.K. to India and Japan, metrosexualmania was everywhere, showing up in newspaper headlines and on the morning TV shows and becoming a hotly debated topic in living rooms and on the street. When you have a story to tell, spend the extra time necessary to come up with an encapsulating term that will capture the public's imagination. It's difficult to imagine a more powerful accelerant. *Metrosexual*? It ended up being named "Word of the Year" in 2003 by the American Dialect Society.

KEEP YOUR BRAIN—AND GOOD JUDGMENT—IN GEAR

Marketers love this quote from American scientist and activist Linus Pauling: "The way to get good ideas is to get lots of ideas." We've used that quote ourselves. What many people don't realize is that the quote goes on to say, "*and throw the bad ones away.*" Failing to do so can lead to some pretty horrific consequences. Yes, *Aqua Teen Hunger Force*, we're talking about you. In the post-9/11 world, it's never a bright idea to place devices resembling bombs beneath highway underpasses or on city street corners. Granted, you got lots of attention—but along with it came $1 million in fines to cover the cost of the police response and another $1 million to smooth over the public with a "goodwill" donation to Homeland Security. Other things to avoid: hiring a tutu-clad imposter to crash an event at the Olympic Games (goldenpalace.com), circulating coupons for free products when there's every likelihood the coupons will go viral and

overwhelm your ability to meet the obligation (Starbucks, KFC), and trying to set the record for the world's largest frozen Popsicle on the first day of summer (Snapple). The latter buzz promotion resulted in 17 tons of bright red goo flooding the streets of San Francisco, leading one nearby worker to muse, "When I saw all those engines I thought it was a huge fire, but it was just a Popsicle." Bottom line: Avoid bunker mentality. Think of what's happening in the world outside your company's walls. Consider all the ways in which the power of a buzz campaign can backfire. And recognize that if something does go wrong, it's likely to do so in a really big, really loud, and sometimes really sticky way.

BE TRANSPARENT AND TRUE

Think of social media as an enormous spy network or high-tech truth detector. It may take a while, but people (or brands) who pretend they're something they're not online always get caught eventually. LonelyGirl15 had a pretty good run, but even she ultimately was uncovered as the creation of a television production company. It took far less time for the guy behind alliwantforxmasisapsp.com to be unmasked as a professional blogger hired by Sony. If you're concerned that the truth coming out will damage your brand, start with the truth upfront. There are no secrets in cyberspace.

**RECOGNIZE THAT
IF SOMETHING DOES
GO WRONG, IT'S
LIKELY TO DO SO
IN A REALLY BIG,
REALLY LOUD WAY.**

VOLVO CARS
"THE MYSTERY OF DALARÖ"

CAN SAFETY BE SEXY?

Volvo has spent decades playing up its safety, a natural selling point for family-car buyers—salarymen, hausfraus, suburbanites. So when the car manufacturer took aim at posh European drivers with its sporty S40, it had a new code to crack. Stylish, sophisticated urbanites in their twenties and thirties dismissed the Volvo marque as stodgy, favoring higher-profile makes such as BMW and Porsche. Those were brands that screamed sex appeal and intrigue. Air bags did not.

Traditional advertising, the standard go-to tool of entrenched marketers with well-established products, fell flat with young urbanites, who preferred the mystique of a cutting-edge purchase. Known to be heavy web users, these tastemakers enjoyed the thrill of the hunt, online and off. To pique their interest, Euro RSCG designed a cat-and-mouse game intended to drive this demographic directly to the client.

The centerpiece of the game, a web film called *The Mystery of Dalarö*, was no *Blair Witch Project*, but its eerie vibe intrigued consumers. The premise: Dalarö, a Swedish seaside resort, gets downright spooky in the off-season, after vacationers have gone home and the boats have been dry-docked. The skies are overcast, the population decreases by half, and the remaining residents start acting, well, strangely. Or so Volvo would have consumers believe.

The eight-minute film documented a single day in October 2004 when 32 families marched into the local Volvo dealership and bought the very same model car. Employing steady-cam and b-roll footage, plus eyewitness testimony, it had all the markings of a documentary. Of course, it wasn't. It was a mockumentary. Spooky footage paired with an unlikely premise drove web users to deliberate its authenticity.

WAS IT A HOAX?
WAS IT A COMMERCIAL?
IT WAS BOTH.

THE MYSTERY OF DALARÖ

In the film, talking heads quoted probability and referenced Carl Jung's theory of the collective unconscious. Buyers gave firsthand testimony: "I think there must be someone in the town with power over minds," one conjectured; "It makes me a little bit afraid of myself—like, what will I do in this car next?" said another before giving a coy smile. And no one had previously heard of the Venezuelan director, Carlos Soto. On the other hand, the film didn't employ the feel-good joyride footage of a typical car commercial. Could it be for real?

To further complicate matters, in the middle of the film a pop-under from Soto appeared onscreen claiming he was duped into making the movie. Clicking on the link launched another film that pointed out inconsistencies in the first. "It was like a Russian doll, a box within a box," says Richard Notarianni, executive creative director, media, Euro RSCG New York.

As preposterous as the premise was, it resonated with consumers. The Volvo website received 750,000 hits. Soto's pop-under lured 85 percent of viewers to click and 60 percent to watch the second film. Supporting media drove the audience to the online experience, while an "unofficial" Soto website created repeat traffic to the official one. Viewers returned to watch *The Mystery of Dalarö* a second time. They began commenting on the film, forwarding the link to family and friends.

Created in Europe by Fuel, a Euro RSCG agency, the film was the brainchild of director Spike Jonze (*Being John Malkovich, Adaptation*). Some argued the film was nonsensical and self-indulgent. Others said it was ahead of its time; had it launched two years later, Notarianni says, Facebook would have turned it into a global phenomenon. Whatever one's views, it was a success. The film was the first of its kind, creating a faux conspiracy, a puzzle for consumers to solve, and a new way for people to spend time with the Volvo brand.

12 MILLION
EXPOSURES IN KEY MARKETS

1 MILLION+
PEOPLE VISITED THE VOLVO WEBSITE

20% OF VISITORS
REQUESTED SALES INFORMATION

TRIPLE-DIGIT INCREASE
IN SHOWROOM TRAFFIC
IN SPAIN, FRANCE, AND BELGIUM

"We moved the conversation of a car launch out of the marketing dialogue and into the cultural dialogue."

—Richard Notarianni, Executive Creative Director, Media, Euro RSCG New York

The Volvo Car Corpora   presents

HOW CAN AN ENTIRE VILLAGE BUY THE SAME CAR ON THE SAME DAY? . . . IT EXCEEDS WHAT COULD HAPPEN

THE MYSTERY OF DALARÖ

ITS REPUTATION AS A SEDATE BRAND ONLY FOR OLDER FOLKS, INJECTING ITSELF WITH A DOSE OF MYSTER

CAMPAIGN PIQUED THE INTEREST OF YOUNG DRIVERS AND CAUGHT THE ATTENTION OF HEAVY WEB USERS

a documentary by
Carlos Soto

CHANCE . . . IS SOME KIND OF UNKNOWN FORCE AT WORK? WITH *MYSTERY OF DALARÖ*, VOLVO UPENDED

ND SEX APPEAL. THE FIRST-OF-ITS-KIND

KEPTICAL OF TRADITIONAL ADVERTISING.

EVIAN
"LIVE YOUNG"

CAN YOU BOTTLE YOUTH?

Anywhere you go, the chemical formula for water is the same: two parts hydrogen, one part oxygen. Water is water. For Evian devotees, however, nothing could be further from the truth. Since its eighteenth-century discovery, Evian water has been renowned for its singular source in the French Alps, its exceptional purity, and its reputation for healthfulness. For hundreds of years, spa-goers have sought out the fabled thermal springs at Évian-les-Bains. Millions of bottles of the water were sold at retail. But by the twenty-first century, lower-priced competitors were springing up, and Evian was losing European market share. The brand needed a rebirth.

THE VOICE OF YOUTHFULNESS

POP VIDEO ERA

Past advertising had focused on the water's authenticity, but that sales pitch was no longer enough. Consumers of bottled water were mostly choosing the cheaper varieties. Even in France, Evian's home market and still its strongest, 54 percent thought the brand was too expensive; 32 percent said they couldn't think of a good reason to buy it. Evian needed to reestablish its raison d'être. But how?

BETC Euro RSCG in Paris knew the target audience was health conscious and intent on maintaining their youth as long as possible. The Creative Business Idea was to marry the brand's legacy as a health water with these aspirations in an entirely new way. In France, expectant and young mothers bought the water for its exceptional purity, good for the kiddies. In export markets, Evian's presence in the world of sport—chugged courtside by Andre Agassi, for example—reinforced its reputation as a restorative agent. Longer life expectancies and the intensified desire for vitality in old age meant the brand message would have to be more pointed than just health. Evian would become the voice of youthfulness—literally.

The core of the agency's 2003 "Voices" campaign was a video recording of the Queen single "We Will Rock You" depicting adult office workers and athletes lip-synching music clearly being sung by children. An onscreen message read, "Drinking pure, balanced mineral water every day keeps your body young." "We tried to reinforce the message that youth is not only a question of age but a state of mind—and body. You have to take care of your youth at every age," says Evian account manager Marielle Durandet. With a clear visual reference to the brand on the jacket, Universal Music released the track as a single. It sold 600,000 copies.

A video clip, "Water Boy," soon followed; in it an animated boy, formed from a drop of water, sings the Queen song while walking through rain, dipping into a glass of water, and hopping through puddles. The clip ran online and was picked up by European music video channels. Children loved the track and the video, and "We Will Rock You" became a schoolyard anthem.

This innovative combination of a television ad, a CD, and a music video placed Evian at the vanguard of advertainment, as early as 2003.

EVIAN'S "WE WILL ROCK YOU" SINGLE SOLD 600,000 COPIES WORLDWIDE.

SOCIAL MEDIA ERA

Five years later, in 2008, Evian faced another hurdle. This time a global recession was denting demand for the premium water, and environmental concerns were driving down sales of bottled waters in general, but Evian couldn't lower prices because of high export costs. The brand needed to reinforce its youthful message in a way that would grab consumers' attention.

Aware of the stakes, BETC Euro RSCG decided to let loose improved technology on a concept it had used with great success years earlier: its "Water Babies" ad, featuring babies performing water ballet. French TV audiences had loved it, going so far as to write letters of congratulations to the Paris office and calling television stations to acquire copies of the

film. For its new iteration, the agency created the blockbuster hit "Roller Babies." As with the first film, it was preceded by the line, "Let's observe the effects of Evian on your body." The 2009 film showed computer-animated babies skate-dancing to the iconic hit single "Rapper's Delight"—cruising, jumping, flipping, and break-dancing to the hip-hop beats.

Once again, the babies were an instant hit. Within three days of the spot's launch in France and Belgium, television news was giving the brand unpaid media time. It was also becoming a viral phenomenon online, ultimately earning a place in the *Guinness World Records* book as the most-watched viral video ever (as of 2011, 180 million views and counting).

The economic climate continued to hammer Evian in 2009 and 2010, but the message of its "Live Young" strategy, emphasizing the brand's youthful effects, traveled around the world. Parent company Danone sponsored a clinical study demonstrating the youth-preserving benefits of its water, and two new Evian spas were launched, in Singapore and Argentina, inviting guests to indulge in rituals intended to "reveal your youthfulness."

Most important, the campaign gave the brand a warmth that cool mountain waters could not. In engaging the public in a truly enjoyable brand experience, Evian established an emotional connection with consumers and an instant brand association with eternal youth.

AWARDED GUINNESS WORLD RECORD FOR

MOST-WATCHED VIRAL VIDEO IN HISTORY

ON VIRAL CULTURE

"THE BIGGEST CHANGE OUR INDUSTRY HAS UNDERGONE IS THE SHIFT FROM BOUGHT MEDIA TO EARNED MEDIA, FROM BROADCAST TO CO-CREATION."

—Naomi Troni, Global CMO, Euro RSCG Worldwide

"Obviously social media is changing the way brands need to channel conversations, but viral, crowdsourcing, and user-generated creativity are just as impactful as conventional advertising. The fact that anyone, anywhere, can create the next Internet sensation that goes viral through social channels creates an environment where brands have to push further and more deliberately into the world culture."

—Rahul Sabnis, Executive Creative Director, Euro RSCG New York

"Strong brands are human brands. If consumers brands, that's an important first step toward

—Peter Schaefer, Planning Director, Euro RSCG Switzerland

"You want a great example of the new world in which marketers operate? Our 'Roller Babies' spot for Evian was named TV Ad of the Year by *Time* magazine in 2009. Only it never actually aired as a TV commercial in America. That's the power of YouTube. That's the power of social media."

—David Jones, Global CEO, Havas and Euro RSCG Worldwide

"Consumers in emerging markets will leapfrog to a behavior pattern that only leaves room for brands that have a positive peer recommendation. And that peer recommendation is based on how brands behave: what they do and why they do it."

— Andrew Knott, Chief Digital Officer, Euro RSCG Asia Pacific

peak about
rusting them."

WHAT MAKES A GOOD VIRAL CAMPAIGN?

Buzz has been a potent force for as long as people have communicated, but social networking's ricochet effect has amplified its power, even as the decline of print, television, and radio has made it more vital. What matters now is motivating the messengers—giving people a reason to post a photo on Flickr or talk about something on Facebook or Twitter. Of course, there's no simple formula to this—unpredictability is in the very DNA of viral messaging. But from our hits (and misses), here are a few lessons we've picked up along the way.

Create an emotional payoff.

Good viral thrives on the relationship between sender and recipient. People will share things that make others laugh or gasp or cringe or cry. The Evian "Roller Babies" video (see pages 42–45) became a YouTube sensation because, as it turns out, there are few things funnier or more adorable than chubby-legged babies doing an alley-oop or acid grind.

Don't overproduce. It may be

about being clever, but it's not always about being slick. Most often, the more real the better. Just ask Scottish singer Susan Boyle: Had she been a gorgeous, perfectly dressed and coiffed performer, would the *Britain's Got Talent* audience have reacted with such emotion and support? Not a chance. People like an underdog, and they also like people and brands they can relate to. T-Mobile's flash mob dance performance at Liverpool Street Station in London has been viewed around 3 million times on YouTube because it is about everyday people and enthusiasm rather than perfection. It features a mishmash of songs, and the performers pull in spectators, getting everyone involved. The blog GeekSugar put it nicely: "It's rare when commercials make you feel good, and even rarer when they can make technology seem like a community enhancer rather than a discourager." Let's face it: It's fun watching elderly women get their groove on.

Protect your flanks. Once it's out there, a viral campaign moves at breakneck speed—and often in unexpected directions. Be prepared to deal with negative reactions, whether it's unhappy customers, calls for a boycott, or just scattered Internet flaming. When General Motors uploaded footage of its new Chevy Tahoe SUV and invited consumers to create their own ads for it, you can bet they weren't expecting eco-minded consumers to create literally thousands of ads attacking the company for contributing to global warming. GM should have constructed the promotion in such a way that it retained more control over what was released to the public.

Say your mea culpas. If your promotion is an epic failure and an apology is warranted, own up to the problem, take responsibility, fix it *fast*, and repeat as needed. Absolut Vodka ran a print ad in Mexico (Absolut Reconquista) that showed an "idealized" map of North America with a portion of the United States returned to Mexico. The reaction north of the border was much as you would expect, and Absolut's "We're sorry if you were offended" response went over just as

well as it does when husbands try it. What should they have done to minimize the damage? Apologize sincerely and pull the ad right away, rather than waiting until the situation worsened. Anti-immigration groups and others called for boycotts, and conservative pundits had a field day over the Swedish company's supposedly anti-American views. Meanwhile, made-in-the-U.S.A. SKYY Vodka took advantage of the situation by reiterating its homegrown roots and announcing its full support of the 1848 Treaty of Guadalupe Hidalgo, which ended the Mexican-American War and gave the United States control over the "Golden West."

Make it last. By its nature viral is fleeting, but the best campaigns have follow-ups ready to go when the buzz dies down. T-Mobile followed up on its dance video with a sing-a-long at Trafalgar Square (4 million views). And Volkswagen enjoyed quite a nice run with its "Fun Theory" campaign, creating videos of such experiments as turning a set of subway stairs into a working piano (yes, it does motivate more people to take the stairs) and a bottle-recycling center into an arcade game (you guessed it: more bottles recycled). All the videos could be viewed on YouTube or at TheFunTheory.com, where visitors were invited to submit ideas for new experiments and vie for cash prizes.

MORTEIN
"MODERN-DAY
RAMAYANA"

HOW DO YOU REACH A MASS AUDIENCE WITHOUT MASS MEDIA?

Television advertising in India is not the communications weapon it is in other parts of the world. In Indian cities, where income is higher and jobs are abundant, most families own a television. But in parts of rural India, where the flat-world revolution has not yet come to pass, less than 35 percent of homes own a television, and electrical blackouts are common. That's a big issue for marketers given the sheer scale of the country and the fact that more than 70 percent of its population resides in rural areas.

THE BRAND TEAM
NEEDED TO GET
VILLAGERS TALKING.

In 2005, Reckitt Benckiser's Mortein was already the number one pest-control brand in Indian cities, thanks in part to a heavy dose of television advertising. Its next target was rural India, where poor sanitation and healthcare make pest control essential to combating mosquito-borne illnesses such as malaria. The issue: how to reach people in the absence of mass communication. If Mortein was to sell its mosquito coil to Indian villagers, it would have to reach them in the most elemental way.

Euro RSCG India understood the challenge. India is a country of complex demographics—six major religions, twenty-nine major languages, at least ten ethnicities, and a lingering caste system. To cut across these divisions, the agency would have to create a grassroots campaign sufficiently engaging to be spread by word of mouth. And that's when a local insight sparked a Creative Business Idea: giving an ancient ritual a modern function. Without hit television shows as a universal source of after-dinner entertainment, the retelling of Indian folklore persists. These centuries-old myths and fables are familiar ground for villagers and, the agency thought, the perfect way to communicate Mortein's role in village life. To tap the rural market, Euro RSCG would recast Mortein mosquito coils

as the victor in the ancient Sanskrit epic tale of "Ramayana." In the retelling of the story, Mortein would take the role of Rama, the seventh incarnation of the god Vishnu. In the role of Lord Rava, the villain who kidnaps Rama's wife, Euro RSCG cast a giant replica mosquito, nicknamed Louie.

In order to tell the story before the biggest audience possible, the agency staged an event at Asia's largest cattle fair, the Sonepur in India's Bihar state, attended by more than 600,000 people annually. The team erected a 50-foot effigy of Louie on the fairgrounds: a blue mosquito in a vest standing upright in a defiant pose. After advertising the event in movie theaters and presenting the story at the fair with actors, Mortein's hero-sized mosquito coil felled Louie with a flaming arrow, destroying the dread disease carrier in a burst of fire.

The buzz surrounding the event drove awareness of Mortein and its mosquito coils, raising the brand's market share 13.5 percent in Bihar, significantly outpacing the nationwide 8 to 9 percent growth that year. The burning of Louie became a fair favorite for three years running. The formerly urban brand had found its way into rural homes without the pervasive power of television.

DRAMATIZING ONE
OF THE MOST POPULAR
TALES IN INDIAN
MYTHOLOGY CREATED
A VIVID STORY LINE
THAT RESONATED WITH
THE RURAL AUDIENCE.

DOS EQUIS

"THE MOST
INTERESTING
MAN IN
THE WORLD"

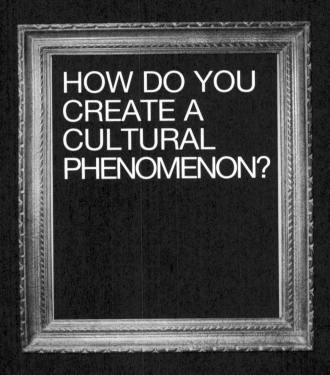

HOW DO YOU CREATE A CULTURAL PHENOMENON?

In 2007, Dos Equis was a small Mexican beer company with two strikes against it in the U.S.: It was largely unknown outside the Southwest, and its nearest import rival was outspending it 3 to 1. With beer losing ground to wine and spirits, the brand needed a fast infusion of magnetism.

GET THE MOST INTERESTING MAN IN THE WORLD TO OFFER INSIGHTS THE WORLD CAN DRINK TO

on PEOPLE

SOME PEOPLE KNOW
MORE *than* YOU.
LISTEN *to* THOSE PEOPLE.

on HAPPY HOUR

HAPPY HOUR *is the* HOUR AFTER
EVERYONE *from* HAPPY HOUR *has* LEFT.

on INSPIRATION

I'VE DONE SOME *of my*
BEST THINKING
on BAR STOOLS.

on CAREERS

FIND OUT WHAT *it is* IN LIFE
THAT YOU *don't* DO WELL *and*
DON'T DO *that* THING.

on BEING BORING

BEING BORING *is a* CHOICE.
THOSE MILD SALSAS *and* PLEATED
KHAKIS DON'T BUY THEMSELVES.

Dos Equis had a few things going for it, including a slightly underground "in the know" appeal and the mystique of its XX logo. What it didn't have was a strong brand identity that would attract the target audience: twenty-something guys, a fickle lot who were known to switch among as many as a dozen beer brands a month. The brand team needed a way into those guys' hearts—and wallets. And they found it by uncovering a deceptively simple insight: "More than anything else, these guys want to be seen as interesting," says Mary Perhach, former chief communications officer at Euro RSCG New York and group account director for Dos Equis. "Guys want to see themselves—and be perceived by others—as standing out from the crowd. Most beers tap into this consumer need. But domestic beers make them stand out because they are outrageous or inappropriate. Our guy wants to stand out because he is interesting."

The category exploration revealed advertising that fell decidedly flat. TV commercials typically spoke to the lowest common denominator, focusing on buxom blondes, sports, and dumbed-down humor (farting horses, anyone?). The ads assumed young guys were utterly unsophisticated, with no interests beyond babes, b-ball, and brewskis. Premium beer drinkers were looking for more.

A Creative Business Idea was born: Dos Equis is the premium beer for those who want to live a more interesting life. "Where competitor brands were holding up a mirror to guys, depicting their lives as one long frat party," says Perhach, "Dos Equis would hold up a lens—letting them see how life could be if they were to live it in a more interesting way."

Enter The Most Interesting Man in the World (MIM), a cult figure created to capture drinkers' imaginations—and aspirations. The silver-haired sexagenarian with Ernest Hemingway's rugged good looks, Hugh Hefner's way with the ladies, and James Bond's taste for adventure was introduced in niche markets in which Dos Equis' sales were strongest. The gentleman was the antithesis of dullness and banality. "He is a lover, not a fighter. But he is also a fighter, so don't get any ideas," warned one TV spot. Commercials featured grainy footage of the MIM rescuing bears from traps, foxes from hunters, and treasure chests from the sea. Oh, and he surfs. Each ad, along with the campaign website (StayThirstyMyFriends.com), served to enrich his aura. Copy, called *legend lines* by the client-agency team, did the same: "He's been known to cure narcolepsy just by walking into a room." "He went to a psychic once…to warn her." "He can speak French…in Russian." Seated at a banquette surrounded by beautiful women, the MIM turns to the camera at the end of each spot to admit, "I don't always drink beer, but when I do, I prefer Dos Equis." Ending with the tagline, "Stay thirsty, my friends."

By inviting visitors to post videos and comments, the website helps build the Most Interesting Man mystique.

Time magazine names the campaign one of the top ten TV ads of 2007.

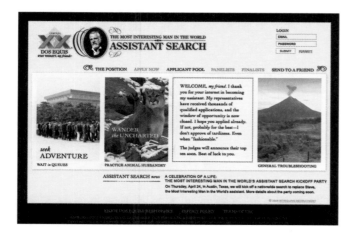

In 2008, the online search for the MIM's assistant attracts more than 3 million hits.

Dos Equis becomes the first beer brand to exceed 1 million likes on Facebook.

Audiences loved him. The campaign took on a life of its own, as fans began creating their own spots and posting them to YouTube. Consumer-generated legend lines appeared all over the Internet: "He is Victoria's Secret." "He has the ability to see black and white... in color." And references to the ads sprang up on TV, including in programming on ESPN and CNBC and on *Late Night with Bill Maher*, *Saturday Night Live*, and *The Daily Show*. Dos Equis fed the enthusiasm, taking the campaign national and creating a Facebook page to keep the legend growing. When the agency team posted a "Help Wanted" ad for the MIM's assistant in 2008, they were inundated with more than 9,000 applications.

The campaign succeeded in reaching beyond the usual beer-category antics, giving the target audience not just a hugely entertaining cult figure but also a persona and lifestyle they could admire. "So many ads for beer and spirits play on a young guy's desperate quest to hook up with the hot chicks at the bar," Seth Stevenson wrote on Slate. "The Dos Equis ads... opt instead for an appeal to dudes' self-conception, placing the focus on older gents who serve as models of masculinity."

Consumers rewarded the campaign by giving back a piece of themselves, in their legend lines, parody videos, and active involvement on the website—and also by buying beer. Since the campaign launched, sales have been up 20 to 30 percent every reporting period. The ad community rewarded the agency with gold, including a Cannes Lion, One Show pencil, and ANDY and Effie awards.

The Most Interesting Man in the World is justifiably proud.

RESULTS

ONE OF THE TOP-PERFORMING CAMPAIGNS IN HISTORY

Sales up 20 to 30%

Most fan'd beer brand on Facebook

A genuine viral campaign created by consumers took flight

Winner of gold awards at Cannes, the ANDYs, the Effies, and London International Awards

Campaign quoted on
ESPN • CNBC
LATE NIGHT WTH BILL MAHER
SATURDAY NIGHT LIVE
THE DAILY SHOW

STAY THIRSTY
my FRIEND

RECIPE FOR A WINNING WEBSITE:
1 PART STICKY, 2 PARTS BOUNCY

{

So you've hit viral nirvana with a video or story or promotion or contest that is so intriguing, so electrifying, that people are flocking to your website. Now what? Here are a few pointers for what to do with those people and how to keep them coming back.

Feed them. Never underestimate the power of conversational currency. People have always loved to have things to talk about, and that has only intensified in the digital age. Give them plenty of content to work with. At VolvoCars.com, visitors can watch video extracts from *LIV* magazine about some of the world's most fascinating people and places, and experience music from Sweden's up-and-coming bands. In advance of the launch of the all-new Volvo S60 in 2010, Euro RSCG 4D Amsterdam wasn't permitted to show photos of the actual car, which was to remain secret until the debut; instead they created a two-part video documentary about a Turkish painter, Esref Armagnan, who, blind since birth, was invited to experience the car via touch and reproduce his image of it in a painting. Thanks to viral spread, tens of thousands of people viewed both videos, and the painting was subsequently sold, with proceeds benefiting the World Blind Union.

Put them at the center of the action. Mountain Dew's DEWmocracy was a seven-stage, yearlong program that invited thousands of the soft drink's most loyal fans to create a new flavor. Using a variety of social networks, including Twitter, Facebook, and YouTube, the promotion involved participants in every stage of development, from flavor and color to naming and package design. When the three new products voted in were ready to hit store shelves, the online fan base was even invited to collaborate in creating the television ads.

Soften the hard sell. Even when the intent of the site is commercial, it typically is better to let the brand or product be a supporting player rather than taking on the star role. Schick sponsored "Clean Break," an online action series centered on sports that, like the new Schick Hydro razor, deliver "unexpected hydration" (think surfing, wakeboarding, and river rafting). The focus was on two athletic buddies, Brady and J. J., and their sporting adventures. Not a razor in sight. Viewers came back to the YouTube channel to catch the latest episode, not to learn about male grooming, but Schick's messages still made it through.

Teach them. Today's consumers are hungry for information—especially when it makes life easier or more satisfying. At Kraftrecipes.com, visitors can attend "cooking school," watching videos with step-by-step recipes and tips, and even inputting ingredients they have on hand in order to call up recipes that feature those items. In the Community section, cooks can exchange recipes, upload images of their favorite dishes, join discussion groups, and post their own blog essays. The trick is to combine elements in such a way as to create a site that is both "sticky" (keeping people there) and "bouncy" (making it easy for them to share content with others). That's what keeps the buzz alive.

REINVIGORATING BUSINESSES AND BRANDS

REMEMBER THE FIVE-YEAR PLAN? In today's environment, it's difficult to imagine anyone putting much credence in a plan that looks that far into the future. New category killers can explode onto the scene without warning and from any direction. Electric typewriter, meet the PC. *Encyclopedia Britannica*, meet Wikipedia. How relevant were Yahoo!'s well-laid plans once Google came online? What is rewarded today is not so much longevity or tradition as agility and a willingness to rethink the business and reinvent the brand. Standing still is a risk no company can afford to take.

McDonald's has been winning the fast-food wars because it has successfully adapted its menu and other offerings to suit consumers' changing wants and needs: an expanded dollar menu for a recession-pounded public, premium items (e.g., McCafé espresso drinks, Angus Third Pounder) for the growing cadre of foodies, health-conscious salads and sides for the anti-obesity brigade, and free Wi-Fi for everyone.

Apple struggled to gain share against Microsoft in the personal computer category, then switched gears, completely reinventing the music industry with the iPod and iTunes before going on to disrupt the mobile phone category with the iPhone. In the process it gained ground in the PC market. Next came the iPad, threatening the market for laptop and netbook computers. Is it any wonder the *New York Times* has labeled Apple an "innovation factory"? The company doesn't just respond to market shifts; it drives these shifts—and in doing so it ensures that its competitors are constantly playing catch-up.

Helping clients to rebrand and reinvent themselves is an increasingly large part of the job of communications agencies. The value of a brand grows or shrinks in tandem with its reputation—how people perceive the brand's relevance, worth, and future prospects. Since the 1980s, Euro RSCG has been using its proprietary Brand Momentum tool to assist clients with strategic planning and product development. The survey tool tracks public perceptions of client and competitor brands, paying particular attention to two dimensions: dynamism and trust. A brand's dynamism is measured by its "movement," encompassing such things as new product lines or packaging, breaking news stories— basically anything that drives buzz and keeps the brand top-of-mind. Trust is measured by the confidence people have in the brand to do what it says it will do and what is right; factors that come into play include product reliability and durability, transparency, customer service, historic roots, and social responsibility.

In the absence of dynamism, even the most trusted brands will wither on the vine. In the absence of trust, dynamic brands may get attention, but actual buyers will be few. To gain or maintain a position as a dominant player in any category requires constant innovation and repositioning (mostly subtle, sometimes major), building on people's trust while also relentlessly pushing the brand forward in new and fresh ways. With Ecomagination, GE gained a new positioning and point of focus, bringing a historic brand firmly into the future. In 2000, when Procter & Gamble announced its goal of acquiring 50 percent of its innovations from outside the company, it opened up all sorts of possibilities for external collaboration, leading to lucrative products and lines such as Olay Regenerist, Clairol Perfect 10, and the Oral-B Pulsonic Toothbrush. No one would ever accuse P&G of standing still.

In this chapter, we look at eight companies in businesses as diverse as automaking and confectionery, auctioneering and fashion. In each case, the agency team shoved aside "business as usual," working with clients to breathe new life into brands—and businesses—in danger of losing relevance.

"A new brand is all promise and vision. Then a market develops and the brand builds trust by delivering on its promises. But the natural cycle of brands means that, left alone, it cannot maintain momentum. In the absence of innovation and dynamism, it ceases to meet the needs of its customers. Brands require tending. A static brand is a dying brand." —Naomi Troni, Global CMO, Euro RSCG Worldwide

THE
SLEEP NUMBER
STORE

By Select Comfort®

CAN YOU SELL SLEEP?

Select Comfort was hurting. The company had been selling its revolutionary air-system mattress for years via direct marketing ads on late-night television. The pitch couldn't have been simpler: The adjustable Select Comfort mattress alleviates back pain. But the product's primary audience—older people suffering through *The Tonight Show*—was simply not buying enough beds to keep the company afloat. Select Comfort's newly arrived CEO Bill McLaughlin challenged Euro RSCG in New York to come up with a campaign that would literally save the business.

THE KEY WAS TO THINK BROADER THAN BACK PAIN.

People aged 55 and up comprised only 21 percent of the U.S. population in 2001, and only a fraction of those consumers suffered the kind of chronic pain Select Comfort's ads were addressing. The agency team decided to stop thinking about back pain and start thinking about what people really want from their mattresses: a good night's sleep. "We wanted to be in the sleep enhancement business," says Rich Roth, co-executive creative director at Euro RSCG New York.

The new target would include younger people aged 25 to 54 with incomes of at least $50,000. These were active adults leading busy lives, able and willing to spend more than $1,000 for some solid shut-eye—"people who are always looking for ways to make their lives better via new technology and gadgets," explains Euro RSCG co-executive creative director Phil Silvestri. And Select Comfort had just the product to appeal to them: a system of adjustable air chambers that allows the user to personalize the mattress's firmness.

With the new target identified, Euro RSCG had to come up with a way to communicate Select Comfort's tech appeal without actually calling the product an *air mattress*, a term that connotes an inflatable bed reserved for overnight guests, not the master bedroom. And they wanted to do it without resorting to the usual mattress-advertising images of happy sleepers nestled under covers and jumping on beds.

After much brainstorming, the team realized the focal point of the campaign was sitting right in front of them: a concept about "Sleep Numbers" first created by the agency in 1997 but never fully developed.

Once a user adjusts the Select Comfort mattress to his or her taste, the digital remote control registers a number between 0 and 100. This is the user's "Sleep Number"—and what the agency would now promote as the "secret to a perfect night's sleep." TV and print ads showed people of all ages and demographics lying in bed, with copy that read, "I'm a 10" or "I'm a 45"; even couples sharing a bed could have separate adjustments. "We never even mentioned we were selling mattresses," Roth says.

It wasn't just the advertising that changed: Every aspect of communication was redesigned to focus on the Sleep Number. The retail locations were rebranded with the Sleep Number name and Sleep Number wall coverings, promotional materials, and signage. And company executives got on board, too, redesigning their business cards and letterhead to feature their own personal Sleep Numbers.

The patented digital remote control had never been named or leveraged as anything more than a product feature.

Euro RSCG made the "Sleep Number" the center of the campaign.

The company needed a 20 percent sales increase to stay in business. "We had to have something that was going to work right from the beginning," Roth says. The agency did even better, boosting sales 30 percent in Sleep Number markets. Inquiries spiked 38 percent, and, amazingly, in its first year awareness of the Sleep Number brand surpassed that of the 14-year-old Select Comfort brand by more than 2 to 1. In 2001, Select Comfort became profitable for the first time in a decade.

HOW DO YOU MAKE OLD SCHOOL NEW AGAIN?

Tennis stars, it turns out, have a long history of being flashy. Long before Serena Williams shimmied into a Lycra body suit, French player René Lacoste threw off the game's traditional linen button-down in favor of his own invention: a short-sleeved polo shirt made from cotton piqué. In 1933, he began mass-producing the shirts, each emblazoned with a trademark crocodile. The brand gained traction as sportswear for tennis players, golfers, yachtsmen, and the rest of the athletic leisure class, landing on American shores in the 1950s. But half a century later, the brand's reputation as cutting-edge sportswear was lost, with the apparel mostly relegated to the dresser drawers of middle-aged country clubbers. Somewhere between René and Serena, Lacoste had lost its mojo.

Monsieur Lacoste was reintroduced as both a sporting champion and an aspirational figure.

AS A PERFORMANCE BRAND,
Lacoste and its cotton piqué had ceded the forecourt to the likes of Nike and Adidas, whose wicking fabrics and nanotechnology made cotton seem quaint. As a fashion brand, it had soared in the 1970s and 1980s, when preppy chic was de rigueur among rich kids and their emulators. Beginning in 2001, designer Christophe Lemaire reworked the line to incorporate modern cuts and bold colors, but the brand was having trouble shaking its dusty image, particularly among young men who didn't read fashion magazines.

To bring Lacoste firmly into the present, BETC Euro RSCG reached into the company's past.

Founder Lacoste could represent everything brand Lacoste wanted to stand for. And while it could no longer compete as performance sportswear, its breezy fabric and comfortable cuts would help young shoppers cast off their high-fashion shackles in favor of a timelessly cool, casual style. Lacoste had a brand heritage far richer than those of its fashion competitors. It was time to take it to market.

The agency's line *"Un peu d'air sur terre"* ("A little bit of air on earth") aimed to communicate this new laid-back attitude. Monsieur Lacoste was reintroduced as both a sporting champion and an aspirational figure, an icon who telegraphed

un peu d'air sur terre

LACOSTE

dynamism and easy confidence. New ads showed him in profile or leaping athletically, and young models dressed in the brand's slimmest, most modern silhouettes were captured in similar midair poses. Taken together, they demonstrated a sense of fun and ease of movement, a cooled-down style that steps away from the fashion hysteria that grips other luxury brands. On the company's website, the idea of weightlessness was played up with images of a "floating" Pong game, a selection of airy music to download, and a contest to win a turn in a zero-gravity chamber. The company also sponsored its heritage sports—tennis, golf, and sailing—as well as athletes such as American tennis star Andy Roddick who embody the brand values.

The global campaign reinforced the change that had taken place in Lacoste's line, communicating a consistent, strikingly contemporary brand image. Consumers stopped seeing the clothing as an old man's weekend wear and began to see it as young and trendy. Buzz rippled through the fashion press, and Lacoste added a second show in New York for its 2006 fall and winter collections.

An Ipsos study revealed that more than 90 percent of consumers liked the ads, and more than 60 percent of 18- to 24-year-olds said they would purchase Lacoste clothing based on the campaign. Sales jumped an estimated 11.5 percent in 2006 over the previous year. Advantage: Lacoste.

LACOSTE HAD A BRAND HERITAGE FAR RICHER THAN ITS COMPETITORS.

ON BRAND MOMENTUM

"In a connected world, the global brand is a shared social currency that must be coherent from place to place and essential wherever it resides. While the instinct of every local creative is to add a new stripe, a different tone, or a bit of native swagger, the successful global brand discovers new relationships and plays in new contexts while always remaining true to itself."

—Richard Notarianni, Executive Creative Director, Media, Euro RSCG New York

"The new consumers are ready to play the 'brand game' to the full, which means that simple, unidirectional, repetitive communication is over for them. Precisely because they are closer to brands and understand them and their role, they want brands to do their job: keep in touch, keep alive, keep being meaningful, keep making a difference, keep the entertainment up, be a good citizen… Makes it really interesting, does it not?"

—Juan Rocamora, Chairman, Euro RSCG Asia Pacific

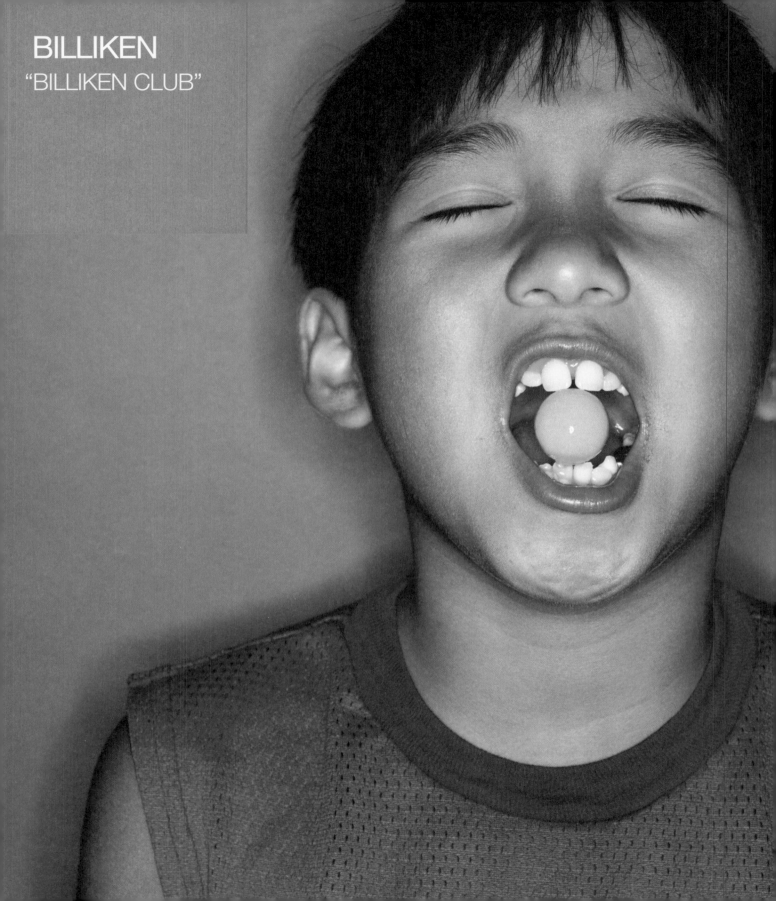

BILLIKEN
"BILLIKEN CLUB"

CAN A SIX-YEAR-OLD RUN YOUR R & D?

Candy makers cater to the most hyperactive impulse buyers around: children hopped up on sugar and looking forward to the next new fix. In Argentina, manufacturers Kraft-Cadbury, Ferrero, and ARCOR launch 150 products every year, hoping to capture kids' fleeting attention with bright packaging and new flavors. Warp-speed innovation is the way to rev up consumer excitement, but in 2001 local candy manufacturer Billiken was about as exciting as unwrapping a vanilla sucker. The 80-year-old brand held nostalgic appeal for parents and grandparents who had loved its hard candies and mints as youngsters. A new generation of candy customers, however, wanted novelty, not nostalgia. Billiken needed a way to connect with kids and ramp up new product production.

To get inside the heads of Billiken's six- to twelve-year-old customers, Euro RSCG in Argentina developed a Creative Business Idea that turned to a natural research and development partner: the kids themselves. While other candy companies were relying on white-coated specialists, Billiken would turn its own target into product designers: "Be part of the dream. You create the candy, Billiken makes it for you." The strategy would entail a seismic shift for the client, a reshaping of its entire process, from product development and manufacturing to package design, marketing, and distribution. But the new strategy also had the potential to create brand loyalty among otherwise fickle youth.

In a series of television ads, children were invited to invent their own candy by registering entries online, then vote for their favorite ideas. The Billiken Club—the first-ever online candy workshop—was born. Children could join the club and draw and submit their ideas on-site. Semifinalist entries were posted and voted on, and the winning candies were promoted in TV ads and at points of purchase. The inventors' names appeared on packaging, further connecting children with the reinvigorated brand.

Billiken's online foray paid off. More than 11,000 entries were submitted in 2001, far more than the 2,500 expected. The website logged 80,000 visitors and 20,000 registered users, much higher numbers than those achieved by even established international brands such as MasterCard, which logged only 5,000 users that year, according to agency research. Moreover, the effort boosted sales 7 percent in the midst of a deep national recession in which confectionery sales dropped 16 percent.

Billiken has repeated the contest every year since. Winning entries have included Aranas, a spider-shaped jelly candy; Que Loco, a lollipop with a powdered center that explodes in the mouth; and Chat, a fruit candy shaped like MSN Messenger icons. Its new brand positioning as a candy by and for children is supported at all points—on television, on packaging, and on kiosks.

Marketers wouldn't coin the terms *crowdsourcing* and *co-creation* until years later, but as early as 2001, Euro RSCG and Billiken discovered the power of handing the factory keys over to the consumer. The strategy transformed the candy company from Grandma's favorite into a vibrant, dynamic brand that gives children a chance to concoct one of their favorite sources of pleasure.

THE CONSUMER AS CO-PILOT

REMEMBER when we had only two choices in our experiences with brands: to buy or not to buy? That almost seems laughable in our radically redefined world. Now actual customers and the interested public have all sorts of ways to involve themselves in a company's business—and the smartest brands are actively encouraging their participation. A few popular approaches:

Brand Ambassador Programs. *Brand ambassador* is a fairly broad term, used to describe any stakeholder who is emotionally invested in growing the business and brand. Now companies are formalizing this natural phenomenon by offering tools, experiences, and incentives to further empower and motivate their consumer evangelists. One example: Green & Black's Organic Chocolate created a Global Ambassadors program to showcase its Fair Trade certification. Ten contest applicants were selected to receive an all-expenses-paid trip to the Dominican Republic, where they spent two weeks learning about the country's cocoa-farming community and the impact Fair Trade has had.

Co-Creation. This is one of those catchall terms that can mean anything from consumers creating designs that a company then turns into products (a system employed by Threadless, CafePress, Zazzle, and others) to companies inviting consumers to create advertising or recommend new or modified products. Lego Factory has become a great source of ideas for the plastic brick–maker. Children use the provided design tool to create and submit ideas in competitions. IdeaStorm is a forum in which Dell computer customers can post, collaborate, view, and vote on ideas for new products and other improvements. In just three years, visitors have generated more than 15,000 ideas, more than 400 of which have been implemented by the company. Dell also holds "Storm Sessions" during which customers submit answers to a single question such as "What's missing from social media?" and "How should we redesign our homepage for at-home users?"

Crowdsourcing. Are many minds—and hands and bodies—better than one or two? Very often, yes. The Genographic Project, a joint venture by National Geographic and IBM to map historical migration patterns around the world, wouldn't be possible without hundreds of thousands of people volunteering their DNA. In 2009, Netflix used the power of crowds to improve its service. It offered $1 million to the person or team who could "substantially improve" the accuracy of its movie recommendations (using past ratings to determine which other movies a user might like). BellKor's Pragmatic Chaos (a combined team from the U.S., Austria, and Canada) created the winning algorithm and walked away with the prize.

In the new digitized, consumer-centric environment, everyone wants a voice, a say, a chance to contribute and influence the businesses they care about. The most effective business ideas will incorporate innovative ways to bring consumers and other stakeholders deeper into the brand process.

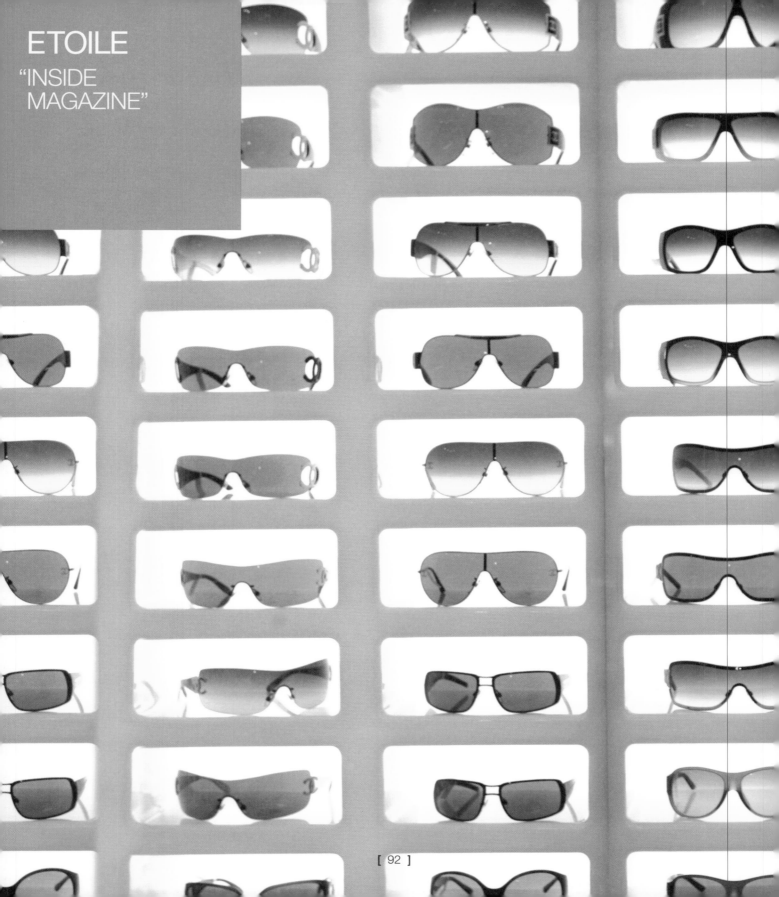

ETOILE
"INSIDE
MAGAZINE"

HOW DO YOU CONNECT WITH A HIDDEN MARKET?

At the start of the twenty-first century, Dubai was a city in ascent. Cranes soared, islands rose from the ocean floor, and ski slopes loomed above the desert. At street level, retail culture also reached new heights. Boutiques teemed with millionaire expatriates and wealthy locals, all looking to indulge. "This is when the fashion industry really picked up on Dubai as the place to be," says Makram Khater, client services director, Euro RSCG Dubai. "The city attracted a lot of deep-pocketed tourists with money to burn."

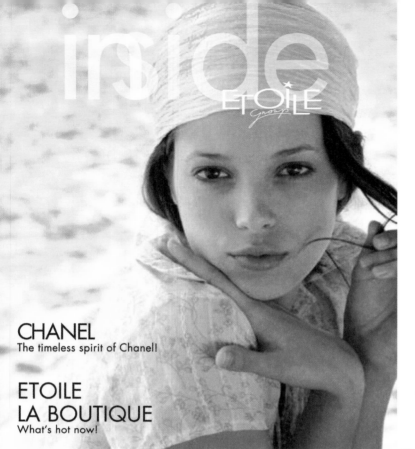

CHANEL
The timeless spirit of Chanel!

**ETOILE
LA BOUTIQUE**
What's hot now!

and Kuwait, the majority of shoppers are Muslim. For them, fashion is a covert affair. "The lady wears an *abaya*, a black cloaklike dress. Underneath is where she wears her haute-couture fashion," Khater explains. "That is why handbags and shoes are the most popular fashion items—over here that is all she shows when she is out in public and in the presence of men." The shoes, the bag, the sunglasses, and the scarf all must pop with color and self-expression.

Fashion houses in Paris and Milan didn't always understand Middle Eastern female shoppers, especially Muslims, leading them to overlook a potentially lucrative market. Etoile needed to convince its retailer clients of the value behind the veils.

The second problem was more practical in nature: how to advertise to these women. In other markets around the world, glossy, fantasy-laden print ads are the surest route to a luxury audience. Think of the

The preferred clientele of many shopkeepers were the big spenders from Russia; stores rushed to stock the showy styles and heavy furs favored by those travelers. But retail group Etoile, manager of boutiques for luxury icons the likes of Ralph Lauren, Chanel, and Valentino, recognized the largely untapped potential of local shoppers. The Kingdom of Saudi Arabia, United Arab Emirates, Bahrain, and Kuwait all brimmed with oil money and luxury-hungry consumers. With the right marketing, Etoile was sure its clients could become the must-have Western brands of the Middle East.

Unfortunately, attempts to pursue this growth strategy smacked up against two seemingly immutable obstacles: First, there was the cultural issue. Style-minded Westerners flaunt their fashion. They want to see and be seen, while on holiday and back home. And while local luxury shoppers in Dubai are a multi-cultural bunch—almost 90 percent of Dubai's population are expatriates—other parts of the Middle East cater to a more traditional community. In Saudi Arabia

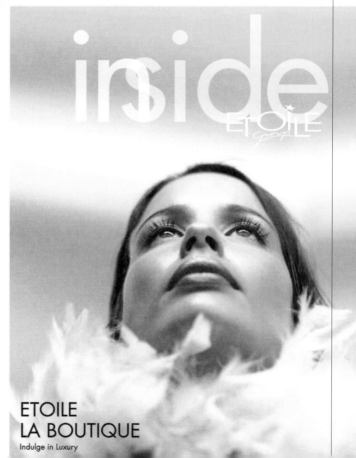

**ETOILE
LA BOUTIQUE**
Indulge in Luxury

> "These women are sophisticated and educated about fashion. People have a misconception that this is a place of uniformity, but nothing could be further from the truth."
>
> —Damien Vernet,
> Louis Vuitton, Middle East

"The results were phenomenal," Khater says. "We were able to release our publication as an insert in high-reach magazines and on its own. Customers actually arrived in our stores magazine in hand."

In 2008, when the global economy crashed, Western luxury buyers tucked away their wallets. But locals continued to spend, inspiring European and North American retailers to look toward the Middle East for new customers. Bloomingdale's announced plans to open a 54,000-square-foot store in the Dubai Mall. Likewise, many of the United Kingdom's leading retail names, including Debenhams, Marks & Spencer, and Topshop, began to extend their reach in the Middle East to compensate for slowing growth at home.

"Spending power is the main reason for opening in the Middle East," brand consultant Amanda Burrows told the U.K.'s *Independent* newspaper. "People there love European brands, and the markups can be a lot higher than in your home country. A high-street brand can be seen as a premium label if they get their marketing right."

heft of fashion advertisements in an issue of *Vogue* or *W*. In Dubai, local women's magazines, read by the wives of princes, oil barons, and real estate magnates, should have made advertisers salivate. Instead, the publications lacked the glamorous art direction and packaging to which Western luxury labels are accustomed. High-end fashion executives were reluctant to use them as a forum for their brands.

Euro RSCG Dubai decided to take matters into their own hands. If the local publications fell short, they would create their own high-end, beautifully designed fashion magazine that would serve as a direct link between Etoile's luxury brands and their local audience. *Inside*, a glossy book with fashion-show footage and ads from client brands, launched in 2005. In order to avoid having the magazine placed alongside lesser publications at retail, the agency struck a deal to piggyback it with top-tier Saudi fashion magazines, automatically putting the English- and Arabic-language publication in the hands of big spenders.

Etoile, thanks to the Creative Business Idea hatched by its agency, was already nicely positioned to reach out to new customers in Dubai and elsewhere in the region. Its flagship store, opened later in 2005 in Dubai's Emirates Mall, offered its client brands a central showcase. And *Inside* gave Etoile a platform through which to shape its own brand message.

With this new, broader reach, Etoile itself became a recognizable name in wealthy households. By 2008, the brand was expanding, opening a new boutique location in the Wafi Mall and sponsoring its own fashion show. In bolstering its clients' brand presence and reach, Etoile had created a brand identity of its own. Today, the Etoile Group operates in six countries around the region, hosting fashion shows and representing no fewer than 65 brands. With *Inside* magazine and the company's subsequent expansion, Etoile has elevated the Middle Eastern fashion industry to even greater heights.

HOW DO YOU MAKE 200 YEARS OF HISTORY MODERN?

For two centuries, Peugeot has been moving people forward—on bicycles and motorcycles, in automobiles and race cars. But on the eve of its bicentennial, the company was part of a hobbled automotive industry struggling to make its way forward through a global recession. French car sales had plummeted 16 percent in the last quarter of 2008, despite government incentives to turn in old cars for new, fuel-efficient ones. Peugeot was hardly in a festive mood, but its birthday was coming up. It challenged BETC Euro RSCG in Paris to reinvent it in time for the big day.

COMBINE WORLDS.
MIX IDEAS.
BLEND
TECHNOLOGIES.

WHEN TIMES ARE TOUGH, people need a very good reason to make a major purchase. The scrappage schemes helped lure some people into the car market, but when it came to choosing a replacement, brands such as Volkswagen, with its straightforward pitch—reliable German engineering for a reasonable price—were the ones capturing sales. VW's tagline, "Das Auto" ("The Car"), communicated that "it's a smart choice, a good car that doesn't show off," says Euro RSCG associate planning director Clarisse Lacarrau. Peugeot's automobiles had trouble competing:

brand emblem, the Peugeot lion, was intended to symbolize the strength and flexibility of its steel); it then branched out into tools, bicycles, and ultimately cars. Each new idea built on the technology the company had previously developed; it manufactured its first car, for example, after producing a bicycle with a motorized engine. It even credits itself with having invented the first electric car—way back in 1941.

As they worked to create a game-changing Creative Business Idea for their client, the agency team

A DYNAMIC FILM TOLD THE STORY OF AN EVER-EVOLVING, INNOVATIVE BRAND

Their previous positioning as cars made mainly for the pleasure of driving wasn't relevant anymore—wind in your hair will get you only so far in a recession. Peugeot needed to reposition itself and revamp its outdated image.

To answer the market challenge without straying from Peugeot's French sensibilities, BETC Euro RSCG decided to tap into the brand's history as an inventor and innovator. The company had first emerged in France 200 years ago as a textile manufacturer and then as a metallurgist specializing in steel (its highly recognizable

began to toss around ideas that would play up the twin pulls of Peugeot's commitment to the exhilaration of driving and its serious grounding in technology and innovation. They knew the winner as soon as one of the strategic planners uttered it: "Motion and Emotion." Those words—which became the campaign's tagline—encapsulated the creative tension that drives the brand.

By the time the agency sold Peugeot on the positioning, the economic climate had shifted. While worldwide demand for cars still hadn't returned to 2007 levels, things were picking up.

By August 2009, sales were up 7 percent over the same period in 2008, according to J. D. Power and Associates. The client's goals had shifted, too. No longer did Peugeot just want to survive the recession; it wanted to improve its standing. Peugeot led the field in France, but Continent-wide the brand lagged at number seven. The automaker's new goal was to place in the top five. Peugeot would have to think internationally.

The "Motion and Emotion" campaign was launched mid-January 2010 with a 60-second brand film

breadth of engineering achievements, culminating in its latest innovation, the BBI electric car. It ends with English-language copy: "Combine worlds. Mix ideas. Blend technologies. Peugeot: Motion and Emotion."

To reach the brand's broadened international target, the film aired across Continental Europe and into Turkey, Russia, and beyond. Meanwhile, print ads in French and English appeared in newspapers in ten European nations. Lastly, 50 Peugeot websites worldwide rebranded simultaneously to showcase the new positioning.

ENGINEERING EVERYTHING FROM COFFEE GRINDERS TO BICYCLES TO CARS.

that perfectly communicates Peugeot's chemistry and history. Directed by Michael Gracey, the same creative behind Evian's "Water Babies," and backed by high-energy dance music from French deejay Yuksek, the film begins with a shot of one of the company's first products, a nineteenth-century coffee grinder. The grinder takes off like a helicopter, then bursts apart in midair. In a flash of red and silver light, the explosion of gears transforms into a bicycle. The bike adds a motor, becoming a motorcycle before exploding and re-forming over and over again into newer, more advanced products. The ad telegraphs Peugeot's

"'Motion and Emotion' changed the image of the brand in a really radical way," Lacarrau says. "Our new concept and the energy with which we expressed it showed people an entirely new side of Peugeot. We made them look beyond their previous impressions of the brand and see Peugeot as it actually is." A European study confirmed this shift, indicating that fewer young drivers now consider the brand old-fashioned and that car buyers overall see Peugeot as a much more modern brand. The company that had evolved a coffee grinder into a sports car had in turn, in the eyes of consumers, been transformed.

CAN TRADITION BE NON-TRADITIONAL?

In India, all that glitters is not gold. Once, gold jewelry was the go-to gift for Indian consumers—a traditional favor for women and an investment for the family. But since the nation liberalized its economy in 1991, consumers have found new ways to spend their money, from luxury fashion to electronics and cars.

Luxury goods were siphoning money from the traditional gold market.

"Suddenly, we can't believe the kinds of choices we have," says former Euro RSCG India CEO Suman Srivastava. "Mobile phones, television sets, watches, travel, and all the rest are fighting for attention." Gold was losing ground.

The market for gold wasn't dead, however. Far from it. India's gold market is the biggest in the world, with consumers there buying some 9,000 tons of it a year. "Indian women do not like wearing fake jewelry," Srivastava explains. "To them, 14-carat gold is not real gold. It has to be 18, 20, or 22 carats."

Even so, India's jewelers, who typically design and fabricate their own pieces, found themselves on hard ground as gold fell out of fashion at the turn of the century. In 2006, the volatile price of the precious metal sent sales plummeting 30 percent year over year. Instead of sharing a bountiful market, jewelers found they were fighting each other gold tooth and nail for a piece of the shrinking segment.

The All India Gems & Jewellery Trade Federation wanted to restore gold's luster and cultural cachet.

And it needed to do it across a dense hodgepodge of geographic, cultural, and socioeconomic boundaries. In a country the size and linguistic and cultural complexity of India, only one medium is capable of that sort of broadscale reach: word of mouth. But how to get people talking? What could drive them out of boutiques and electronics showrooms and back into jewelry stores? And what could breathe new life into an industry seen as stale and predictable? The answer: an unprecedented national promotion that would unite some 20,000 gold (and eventually diamond) vendors across the country and give consumers a strong reason to buy.

The resultant campaign was half Creative Business Idea, half military-style mobilization. The Federation and Euro RSCG India joined forces to persuade jewelry retailers to put aside their squabbles and come together for a 45-day sales push planned around the festival of Diwali.

Diwali, a Hindu festival that celebrates the triumph of good over evil, is an occasion for cheer and gift-giving, not unlike the Yuletide shopping period in Western countries. In India, it is particularly auspicious

LUCKY
LAKSHMI

INDIA'S JEWELLERY FESTIVAL

to buy gold during Diwali. Euro RSCG India intended to give consumers even more reasons to do so.

The campaign was called "Lucky Lakshmi"—*Lucky*, because $21 million in prizes would be distributed through scratch-off cards available at participating stores (grand prize: five kilos of gold!); *Lakshmi*, after the Hindu goddess of wealth. Indian women traditionally are considered the Lakshmi of the home. The branding was sufficiently simple to be understood across the country. And the fact that every one of the 25,000 scratch-cards rewarded the customer with at least a token prize was more than enough to stoke excitement among festival-goers.

In addition to navigating the Federation's political rivalries, the agency also had to demonstrate a certain socioeconomic sensitivity. "Gold cuts through all strata of society, from the wealthy to just above the poorest," Srivastava says. "We had to ensure it didn't sound like a promotion for just the wealthy or middle class."

To accomplish that, the agency team put together a cross-country road show that would stop at 250 towns and villages of varying prosperity, as well as 60 hub cities. The effort demanded banners, ads, brochures, invitations, and other materials in nine languages and the coordination of Euro RSCG India's public relations, strategic, and advertising capabilities. Materials were distributed by plane, train, and automobile, with PR localized for the various news outlets.

The event was a hit. Over the course of the festival, jewelry sales reached $70 million, a 40 percent increase over the same period in 2005. The event drew 8,000 more vendors than expected, with an additional 3,500 shopkeepers asking to participate as the promotion got under way. It ended up being not just the largest jewelry promotion in India but the largest anywhere in the world. An industry cast in ancient traditions found a distinctly modern way to shine.

THE ROAD SHOW VISITED 250 TOWNS | **8,000 MORE VENDORS THAN EXPECTED** | **$70 MILLION IN SALES... A 40% INCREASE**

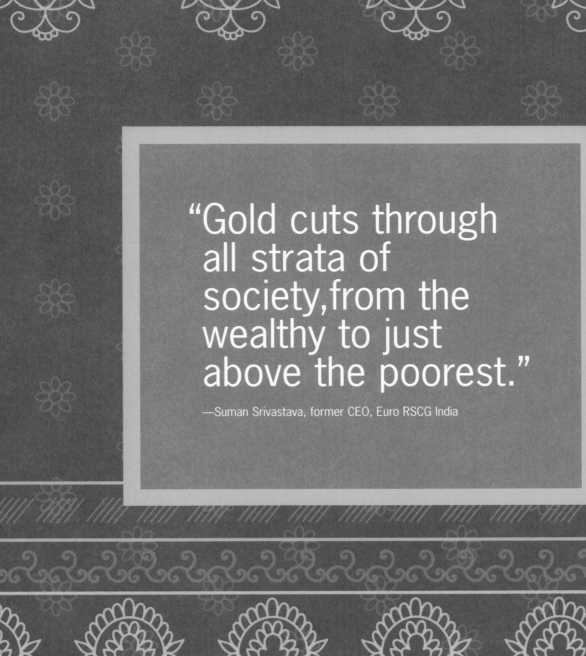

"Gold cuts through all strata of society, from the wealthy to just above the poorest."

—Suman Srivastava, former CEO, Euro RSCG India

YOU ARE **ebaY**™ **.fr**

CAN OLD MEDIA SELL NEW MEDIA?

Vintage bowling shirts with pink piping. Cow-shaped salt and pepper shakers. A 1961 issue of *Paris Match* featuring Brigitte Bardot. In France, as around the world, eBay is the site where shoppers—specialists and collectors, in particular—can find that unique object. In 2007, after seven years in the country, eBay counted more than 10 million registered users in France. But to continue growing, the auction forum needed to convince shoppers to rely on the site for more casual and everyday purchases.

BETC Euro RSCG in Paris began by recognizing that eBay's appeal was very much the same as a flea market, where individuals offer an eclectic array of items. Online shoppers tired of homogenized retail chains couldn't find a better alternative than eBay. Rather than wander aisles filled with mass-produced fashions, an eBay shopper might have the choice of a vintage Chanel jacket offered by Fizzy1986 or a handmade cardigan from GrannyAllStar23. Moreover, the site was a paradise for proactive shoppers, allowing them to hunt down the product they wanted and set the price themselves. Taken together, eBay was the perfect embodiment of Web 2.0: by the people, for the people.

With these shoppers in mind, the Paris team devised a strategy that would put eBay sellers at the center of the action. And they would use an "old" medium—television—to sell this new medium. Armed with the tagline, *eBay, c'est vous* ("You are eBay"), the agency launched what they described as the first-ever 2.0 advertising campaign: They bought airtime for ten television spots and put these spots up for auction on eBay. Any seller could bid for one of the spots, which they would then use to air a commercial for one of the items in their eBay inventory. And not just any commercial—a commercial created in partnership with BETC Euro RSCG, the leading advertising agency in France. An amazing opportunity for the price.

In advance of the auction, the agency ran TV commercials featuring a white space and a revolving cube with the notice, "eBay is putting this ad space up for auction. Come and sell your item on TV."

The top bidders spent between €300 and €2,200 for the spots—which at the time was the equivalent of $430 to $3,175. (Proceeds were donated to the charitable environmental organization Planète Urgence.) The agency worked feverishly with the ten winners, writing and filming two 30-second ads every day for a week. A crew of 80, including copywriters, art directors, film editors, and lawyers, was on the set to ensure a smooth shoot.

The finished ads shared the same all-white art direction, but each had its own character and content. One ad cast an awkward, bespectacled seller in the role of spaceship captain, a story inspired by his coffee table's otherworldly quality. One car seller took his auto for a "spin" in the studio, with white-clad actors representing the wind, rain, and changing scenery outside the car. The ads were aired two weeks after the auction ran and stopped running once the items were sold.

"The eBay auction winners were really excited about the whole thing," associate director Philippe Brandt says. "They got to see an ad in the making, and they were the star of it. For them, selling their items was secondary to being part of an incredible life experience."

SELLERS ENJOYED THEIR 15 MINUTES OF FAME—AND A ONCE-IN-A-LIFETIME EXPERIENCE.

Following the campaign, the site registered a 5 percent increase in bidding, and users were 30 percent more intent on making a purchase than before. Most important, in the months following the campaign, 1 million more users registered online. eBay had been successfully repositioned as a place in which to find everyday bargains and one-of-a-kind essentials, not just a site for collectors.

THE AUCTION ADS SPARKED THE HIGHEST NUMBER OF VISITS TO EBAY'S FRENCH SITE IN ITS HISTORY.

ON GETTING TO THE FUTURE FIRST

"Most agencies, and by extension most companies, are focused on today: how to get ahead or merely stay afloat *today*. Euro RSCG's entire energy is devoted to giving our clients momentum so that they're playing a different game, in a different league altogether from their competition. We're taking them to tomorrow."

—Narayan Devanathan, Chief Strategy Officer, Euro RSCG India

"Taking our clients to the future first means creating shortcuts that will save them time and therefore money. To catch up with trends before their competition and be more insightful and relevant. We make it possible because all our proprietary research tools are forward-looking and predictive, whether it is Prosumer or Brand Momentum and above all Decipher (semiotics). Because we can look forward into the future of categories and decipher their codes before anyone else, our clients' brands will be the brands of the future."

—François de Rivière, Creative Strategy Director, Euro RSCG Southeast Asia

"Getting to the future first means helping our clients be the brand owners that competitors look at and think, 'I really wish we'd done that. That so changes the game. That means we're in trouble.' What could 'that' be? Getting dual shelf placement in supermarkets, a different way of framing a category, a new product idea, a story that gets spread round the world... 'That' is a Creative Business Idea."

—Phil Johnston, Head of Planning, Euro RSCG Sydney

[115]

CAPGEMINI
"COLLABORATIVE
BUSINESS
EXPERIENCE"

CAN YOU LEAD THE PACK BY TAKING A BACKSEAT?

Capgemini Ernst & Young. The name doesn't exactly roll off the tongue, but that unwieldy moniker was the least of the company's worries at the start of the last decade. When Capgemini acquired Ernst & Young in 2000, its ambition was to become one of the top three IT services and consulting companies in the world. The merger was considered a bold strategic move applauded by the market and employees alike, but the timing was unfortunate: The burst Internet bubble and other industry challenges laid low the sector in which the company operated. And when the newly formed organization stood toe-to-toe with big spenders such as Accenture, brand awareness was a challenge.

Four years later, the company was—mercifully—returning to a more streamlined name, jettisoning Ernst & Young in favor of the stand-alone Capgemini. The change opened the door for a brand repositioning campaign.

"It was a depressed market, and morale in the company was low," recalls Mieke Van Handenhove, the Capgemini senior executive in charge of global branding at that time. "The name change was an opportunity to rethink our positioning in a way that was consistent with our brand equity, recognized strengths, DNA, and values and to develop a brand program that would inspire our tens of thousands of employees and make the brand stronger, more distinctive, and more valued in the market."

Euro RSCG C&O was chosen to give the company a much-needed shot of adrenaline. The agency's first step was to hold a series of workshops with top management, while also examining what was happening within the business, in the category, and, most important, among consumers (in this case, corporate clients). The research uncovered a vital insight: Clients no longer wanted to deal with "masters of the universe," consultants who act like managers instead of partners. They were looking for true collaborators and confidants who would assist them with their specialized skills rather than boss them around.

The Creative Business Idea was simple: Capgemini would henceforth be a company that offers the "Collaborative Business Experience™." With just three words, the company had gained not just a fresh way to position its services but also a new way to relate to the market and do its job. Creating a truly Collaborative Business Experience (CBE) would require an approach and mindset unique in the category: The global company would be modest, warm, and technology-neutral, and its offerings would be customized to each client's needs.

The next steps were to spread the word internally at Capgemini and devise a marketing campaign that would work at the global level. The agency achieved these goals with another deceptively simple idea: Capgemini

Research revealed that clients wanted collaborators and confidants rather than managers.

'My first priority? Enhancing his phenomenal capabilities"

TONY VISCONTI
David Bowie's producer

Introducing the Collaborative Business Experience

True talent only comes from within. But today, in music or in business, to achieve success, to build on it and to make sure you keep it, you need collaboration. With someone who inspires, challenges and stimulates you, someone who leaves you better prepared for the future. Someone who will share with you knowledge, practices, risks. And Results. Discover the Collaborative Business Experience, discover Capgemini, a partner on which you can count day after day. A partner who is committed to helping you achieve faster, better and more sustainable results. And puts it on paper.
www.capgemini.com

Capgemini
CONSULTING.TECHNOLOGY.OUTSOURCING

would be "the people behind the people." The agency's initial plan was to create an ad featuring Steve Williams, Tiger Woods's longtime caddy. But the week they were to pitch the concept, Accenture debuted a campaign featuring the famous golfer and characteristically cast themselves in the superstar role—precisely the role Capgemini didn't want to play. "We wanted to be the one in the shadows who helps you be at the top of your market," explains Marc Saint Ouen, partner at Euro RSCG C&O. "You would be the champion, and we would be behind you."

The resultant campaign featured the likes of Darren Cahill, coach for tennis star Andre Agassi; Tony Visconti, producer for David Bowie; and Ralph Vicinanza, literary agent for Stephen King. It raised company morale by giving Capgemini employees pride in their value to clients and a fresh way of thinking about their business. "In a people-oriented business like ours, internal pride and energy is what drives business momentum, and that's exactly what CBE gave us," says Van Handenhove. Extending far beyond advertising, the Collaborative Business Experience became a catalyst for change in the organization, impacting Capgemini's communications and marketing, human resources, sales, and service delivery processes. CBE is more than an internal philosophy; it has led to a set of business tools and methodologies that allow clients to achieve better, faster, and more sustainable results.

Two years after launching CBE, Capgemini's profile was on the rise in North America and Germany, both markets in which the company's image had previously lagged. Top business schools and universities rated the company highly as a prospective employer.

"Today, even though advertising concepts and taglines have evolved, the competitive advantage of our new approach is still recognized by clients and more than 100,000 employees alike. We continue to use the CBE label as a market promise of collaboration," says Philippe Grangeon, Capgemini group marketing and communications director.

The idea was deceptively simple: Capgemini would be "the people behind the people."

"Helping him get results, that's what I'm all about"

DARREN CAHILL
Andre Agassi's coach

Introducing the Collaborative Business Experience

Whatever the situation, whoever the opponent. Today, success in tennis or business is almost impossible without collaboration. You need to work with someone who knows and understands you, someone who listens to what you really need and, with you, defines realistic objectives and the ways to reach them. Someone who will share with you knowledge, practices, risks. And Results. Discover the Collaborative Business Experience, discover Capgemini, a partner you can count on day after day. A partner who is committed to helping you achieve faster, better and more sustainable results. And puts it on paper. www.capgemini.com

CONSULTING.TECHNOLOGY.OUTSOURCING

THINKING BIGGER THAN THE BUSINESS

"SUCCESSFUL COMPANIES base themselves around fixed core values, but at the same time adapt to a world that is in constant motion," ad veteran Jean-Marie Dru said in an interview. He got it exactly right. Brands today must fight a perpetual battle for relevancy, forever adapting to changing markets, new modes of communication, and consumers' growing influence and power.

You don't have to look terribly hard to find examples of businesses that clung to the old ways for too long. IBM is on an upward trajectory today, but it paid dearly for holding firm with computer hardware in the 1980s rather than transitioning straightaway into the high-growth software sector. GM stood still while Japanese automakers reinvented the industry. Barnes & Noble tried to play catch-up with Amazon and the Kindle when it should have been reimagining its place in the world. Likewise, Blockbuster defined itself too narrowly (as a video-rental retailer), thereby leaving the door open to upstart competitors such as Netflix (videos via mail/download) and Redbox (kiosks in grocery stores and other locations). By the time Blockbuster got serious about competing in these new formats, it was facing an uphill climb.

Contrast these struggles with businesses that have grown by more broadly defining their purpose, industry, and competitive set early on. MTV could have positioned itself as nothing more than a cable music video channel; instead, it became a purveyor of pop culture and a platform for youth activism. Moving into nonmusic programming, including reality shows, proved prescient now that music videos are readily available on the web. Its broader positioning and mind-set have given it license to play anywhere it cares to within the youth and young adult arenas. Similarly, ESPN might have defined itself simply as a sports broadcaster; positioning itself as being in the sports enthusiast business instead has enabled it to move into a variety of other mediums, including *ESPN* magazine and books, ESPN Sports Zone (a chain of sports-themed restaurants), video games, and ESPN MVP (a mobile sports-information service in partnership with Verizon Wireless).

Generally speaking, the broader the brand values, the more room there is for a brand to grow. When greeting-card company Hallmark began to feel the effects of competition from "e-cards" and online communication in general, it was able to branch out in new and profitable directions thanks to an already well-established brand essence that embodies family values, including love, tradition, decency, and security. Throughout the past century, this broader ethos has given Hallmark permission to extend its brand into television (first with the Hallmark Hall of Fame specials beginning in the 1950s and now with 24-hour family-friendly programming on the dedicated Hallmark Channel), retail (there are thousands of Hallmark Gold Crown stores), publishing (gift books), ornaments and party supplies, and even, with the help of Euro RSCG, the flower-delivery business. As the company moves into its second century, its core values will continue to offer a platform for growth.

In the same vein, starting with a mail-order music business, Richard Branson has created an empire (in the process becoming one of the world's wealthiest men) by building Virgin Group as an entity based not on any particular product type but on such concepts as innovation, fun, and freedom. That brand essence has allowed the company to move beyond record stores into industries as diverse as mobile telephony, transportation and travel, financial services, media, and fitness. Virgin Group now incorporates more than 300 branded companies, from Virgin Airways and Virgin Holidays to Virgin Gaming and Virgin Money, in 30 countries.

MTV and ESPN, Hallmark and Virgin—each of these businesses created opportunities for growth by refusing to be boxed in by limited thinking. Rather than cling to old business models and a "business as usual" mind-set, they have constantly reassessed what categories and industries they are in, whom their target customers can and should be, and how they should be conducting business. This has kept them a step ahead, always moving forward rather than scrambling to follow the lead of upstart competitors.

In this chapter, we look at six organizations that have evolved their brands by thinking beyond their product categories in a way that has given them room to grow, a new sense of direction, and a fresh and engaging message to communicate.

ON BREAKING OUT OF THE BOX

SOME BRANDS become so strongly associated with a particular product that customers lose sight of the broader offering. Mention Intel and people automatically think microprocessors. But the company is so much bigger than that: Intel is a provider of technology solutions for business. With Intel inside their businesses, not only their PCs and servers, IT managers have a superior IT infrastructure. In Latin America a job in IT management is a strong career option. Formal training and ongoing education, however, are out of reach for many. To help train the next layer of IT managers and create loyalty early in their careers, in 2002 we created the

Intel Next Generation Center, a free online series of workshops that introduced those at junior levels of IT or aspiring to get into IT, as well as business users, to new technologies and assisted in their career advancement. Whether teaching about customer relationship management, information services, or tools for e-business, the center exposed clients and potential clients to the full breadth of the Intel business. Critically, it also provided accreditation, with a certificate, when they completed all 12 modules. It wasn't just a great resource; it was also a consistent reminder of the broader business Intel is in.

—George Gallate, Global Chairman, Euro RSCG 4D

AIR FRANCE
"MAKING THE
SKY THE BEST
PLACE ON
EARTH"

Seat
8B

HOW DO YOU MAKE BUSINESS PLEASURE?

Air France has long stood for everything French—good wine, incomparable cuisine, high fashion, luxury—but in 2000 reality wasn't living up to reputation. Its fleet's interiors were crying out for redecoration and its cuisine was old-fashioned. It didn't offer the in-air services other luxury liners were advertising: no video on demand, no plush seating, no lie-flat beds. And it simply couldn't afford to cut costs steeply enough to compete with the Ryanairs of the world.

From the start, it was clear to BETC Euro RSCG that what was needed went well beyond advertising. The airline required a creative blueprint for change and a new way to think about its business.

Both the airline and the agency focused on the most important ticketholders: business travelers, who account for a disproportionate share of the profits. These travelers are willing to pay a premium for seats and service that ensure they have a restful flight and will be fresh for their meetings. An agency study revealed that those in business class expect not only seamless check-in but also to be the center of attention during flights, doted on by attendants and enveloped in a cocoon of efficiency and comfort. The agency turned that insight into an idea that would change how Air France operates and is perceived.

"We wanted to transform Air France from a simple airline into a true well-being provider," says Claus Lindorff, managing director at BETC Euro RSCG. "We wanted to help our client move beyond providing transport to delivering a transformative experience. It's not just where you're going that matters, it's how you feel when you finally get there."

Making the Creative Business Idea a reality was no simple task. It required a considerable reinvention of the airline, including upgraded services and amenities. "The idea," says Lindorff, "was that a flight on Air France would mirror all the best aspects of traveling 'in the French way': inspired cuisine, fine wines, rich culture, exquisite fashion, and a notion of a certain style." *Nouvel Espace Voyageur* was introduced onboard: an elegantly redesigned space offering the lie-flat seats and personal entertainment travelers craved. Soft wool-blend blankets, slippers, and other personal accoutrements were presented to every business-class traveler, alongside a down-feather pillow and complimentary Champagne. Attendants were fashionably outfitted in uniforms designed by none other than Christian Lacroix, while the cuisine got an overhaul from celebrity chef Guy Martin and wine expert Olivier Poussier. Health-conscious travelers were catered to with lighter snacks that embraced the wellness theme. After dinner, ambient lighting throughout the plane encouraged restful sleep. The agency even designed an in-flight channel devoted to airy, restful music.

Air France was ready to reclaim the luxury travel niche and fulfill its brand promise: "Making the sky the best place on earth." Television advertising efforts focused on the poetry of the tagline, the beauty of travel reflected in a series of restful images—fog on a still lake, swimmers diving into a cool pool. The print ads evoked the beauty of traveling to a unique destination, while suggesting the tranquility to be found onboard. Furthering communication of the wellness message, a mini brand website was designed to set a more relaxing tone and be more user-friendly; it featured spa-style music and a brand film extolling the new onboard amenities.

The overhaul resulted in record occupancy rates: 83 percent of business seats were booked on flights that took off in 2006. Revenues spiked 16 percent in the second quarter of 2006 and 12 percent in the fourth. The ads won both an Epica Silver Award and an outdoor Grand Prix Award that year. Air France had moved beyond a transport company to a company in the business of delivering a wellness experience.

"WE WANTED TO TRANSFORM AIR FRANCE FROM AN AIRLINE INTO A WELL-BEING PROVIDER."

"IT'S NOT JUST WHERE YOU'RE GOING ... IT'S HOW YOU FEEL WHEN YOU FINALLY GET THERE."

RECORD OCCUPANCY RATES IN BUSINESS AND FIRST CLASS

[MORE THAN 1,700 FLIGHTS AROUND THE WORLD PER DAY.]

[1,001 THOUGHTFUL ACTS IN BUSINESS CLASS.]

"THIS IS ADVERTISING. YOU HAVE TO RUB PEOPLE ONE WAY OR THE OTHER. "

—Phil Silvestri, Managing Director/Executive Creative Director, Euro RSCG Tonic

Are you gellin'?®

Dr. Scholl's was in a bind. It was an exciting brand stuck in a category associated in consumers' minds with orthopedic shoes and ankle-puddling support hose. How do you breathe new life into a 100-year-old brand, getting people to see it in a fresh and more flattering light? You don't just reinvent the product; Scholl's had already done that, with a brand-new line of gel inserts. You reinvent the category, taking it out of nursing homes and into dance clubs, removing the stigma of arch supports and varicose veins by rebranding the category as lifestyle supplements rather than medical aids.

HOW DO YOU MAKE AN UNLOVED CATEGORY LOVABLE?

In 2003, faced with declining foot traffic, Dr. Scholl's traded the world of swollen ankles and aching bunions for a walk on the lighter side. Ads for the company's new gel inserts, from Euro RSCG Tonic in New York, featured people whose feet were so deliriously comfortable their owners couldn't help but burst out in rhyme. "Are you gellin'?" one would ask. "I'm gellin' like Magellan," came the answer. The campaign was clever and insidious, and it had legs.

"Are you gellin'?" almost immediately earned a place in the pantheon of modern taglines, alongside such icons as "Whassup?" and "Aflac!" Audiences loved it. And hated it. And loved to hate it. Even as message boards rang out with love notes, a petition began to circulate, calling for the company to yank the TV ads altogether.

"WHY DON'T I JUST PUT ON A WHITE BELT AND GO TO THE DOG TRACK?"
one focus group member asked.

"This country has enough problems," the petition declared. "This shouldn't be one of them." Advertising blog AdFreak advised Dr. Scholl's to "Put a sock in it," while consumers posted parodies on YouTube.

Agency managing directors and executive creative directors Phil Silvestri and Rich Roth couldn't have been more pleased. "People don't think about their feet," says Roth. "We thought that as baby boomers aged, their feet would deteriorate, and there would be more demand for insoles," he says, but he and his longtime creative partner were

[138]

"No tellin' how much I'm gellin'"

"Are you gellin'?"

"I'm gellin' like Magellan"

wrong. The trouble was, youth-obsessed boomers would rather grin through the pain than buy orthopedic inserts. "Why don't I just put on a white belt and go to the dog track?" one focus group member asked.

The agency had to create an entirely new category for the brand, moving away from selling Dr. Scholl's as a solution to foot pain—an old person's problem—and focusing instead on comfort and the lifestyle benefits of feeling good. Then the veteran team worked on infusing their communications with a cooler vibe.

"When you're at a party and you're feeling good, you say, 'I'm chillin',' Roth explains. "In the ads people were saying, 'I'm gellin'.'" Adds Silvestri, "We wanted it to be a code, a sort of secret handshake."

Code? Maybe. Secret? Not so much. "Gellin'" made its way into the cultural conversation within weeks. David Letterman and Jon Stewart played the line for laughs. Ellen DeGeneres wondered why she hadn't been drafted. ("Doesn't it seem like an obvious commercial for me to be 'gellin' like Ellen?'" she asked.) Even *Mad Men* wrote

Dr. Scholl's into an episode—Sterling Cooper loses the account because its work is "dull and humorless."

Roth and Silvestri didn't have that problem. The more attention the campaign got, the more brazen the ads became. The ads went from "gellin' like a felon" to "gellin' and Zinfandellin'," all in 30 seconds. Fans and foes multiplied. Everyone had an opinion. "We recognize that the rhyming thing irritated some people," Silvestri says. "But this is advertising; you have to rub people one way or the other."

Bottom line: The campaign worked. Sales of the gel insoles, already Dr. Scholl's best seller, shot up 100 percent. Other Scholl's insoles got a 25 percent sales boost, and the entire category enjoyed a 15 percent uptick. Most important, a new category of lifestyle-centered foot products was born, allowing the brand to march into its second century with its future lookin' good. Dr. Scholl's? So totally gellin'.

GEL INSOLES SALES ROSE 100%

ARMY
RECRUITING
GROUP

"ARMY ON EVEREST"

CAN YOU BRAND AN ARMY?

At the turn of the twenty-first century, the British Army was taking on heavy fire on the public relations front. Involvement in unpopular wars in Iraq and Afghanistan had tarnished its reputation. Equally damaging was the long-running Deepcut scandal, regarding a pattern of bullying and abuse uncovered at a U.K. barracks. Recruitment figures had fallen dramatically, down to 10,400 of the 14,000 soldiers needed to meet the Army's goals, according to a report in the *Guardian*. The military's image needed some serious buffing.

Euro RSCG recognized that the British public had too narrow a view of its military. It needed to be reminded of the tremendous courage of the combatants, to see the real heroes underneath the uniforms. So when the agency learned the Army was planning to summit Mount Everest via its most difficult route, "We jumped on it," says Holly Ward, former managing director at Euro RSCG London PR. It would be a heroic 8.8-kilometer slog up the West Ridge, where more climbers have died than succeeded. "We realized it was something that could show the training and variety the Army has to offer," Ward explains. "It was a way to remind people of the individuals willing to give everything for their country."

A survey of media outlets found that interest in the event was focused only on a single moment: the final surge to the summit. But the agency saw in the expedition greater potential as an ongoing reality TV drama that would hook audiences with a narrative of adventure and daring over several weeks. Working with the Army's marketing team and ad agency, Euro RSCG London PR helped put together a multimedia campaign that included TV advertising, press feeds, celebrity endorsements,

and a campaign website—armyoneverest.mod.uk—designed to hook the public and press from day one.

To set the stage, the team prepped the media with a series of PR events—including one at Royal Military Academy Sandhurst—at which reporters could interview members of the Army ascent team on whatever topics were of interest, from physical fitness and leadership

Tony Blair broadcast words of encouragement, deejays praised the team on-air, newspapers covered the ascent every day.

skills to the environment and women in the military. The expedition website launch followed, as did appearances by the climbers at outdoor sporting shows, which aimed to get the attention of action-and-adventure enthusiasts. To drum up interest among children, the ascent team appeared on BBC TV's popular children's show *Blue Peter*.

To capture on-the-scene mountaintop excitement, Euro RSCG London PR forged a partnership with Sky News: The news team would actually embed

with the mountaineers, filming regular reports and sending them to London via satellite. After Sky News broadcast its own reports, the agency team edited in additional footage and posted it to the website. "I was in the edit suite most evenings until quite late, sifting through footage," says Ward. "Our aim was to get viewers emotionally invested in the event and in the lives of the climbers. It really helped to be able to show how physically and psychologically invested the news professionals themselves actually were; their experience alongside the soldiers added an extra dimension to our coverage."

The video was gripping: fit young Brits standing at the base of the world's tallest mountain, ready to conquer the world, then scaling sheer snowy walls armed only with pickax and climbing rope. Their wind-chapped faces, ice-crusted beards, and breathless exhaustion in the face of 150-mile-an-hour winds told a tale of deprivation and determination. On-camera interviews drove home the climb's purpose. "We as soldiers need to be able to make decisions in difficult conditions, and this expedition offers the ultimate environment," said Chief Warrant Officer Dave Bunting. Occasionally, while scouting teams ascended

or when weather conditions proved impenetrable, climbers sacked out on the mountain's face in pup tents and lawn chairs, bantering and enjoying once-in-a-lifetime views. The soldiers also supplied daily diary entries, which the agency made available on the expedition's website. Visitors could track the team's progress via a satellite signal, view entries and video, sign up for daily alerts—and, of course, inquire about jobs and training available in the Army.

On the ground, notables such as Tony Blair and Simon Cowell offered words of encouragement, and deejays praised the team on-air. National newspapers covered the ascent daily, and a companion advertising campaign from the Ministry of Defense shared autobiographical footage of the climbers.

Ultimately, the mountaineers did not reach the summit, forced to abandon their attempt due to life-threatening weather and avalanche conditions. "It was the greatest summit that never happened," Ward says. "We were totally devastated, really sad." But the decision to scuttle the climb reflected well on the officers, who appeared as stoic adventurers in the footsteps of Sir Edmund Hillary, whose own ascent was hailed by the British press as a coronation gift

Their wind-chapped faces, ice-crusted beards, and breathless exhaustion in the face of 150-mile-an-hour winds told a tale of deprivation and determination.

for Queen Elizabeth II in 1953. More important, the Army's willingness to put its soldiers' welfare ahead of the mission—which was, after all, about PR and training, not a combat objective—proved a powerful counterpoint to the negative image generated by the recent scandal and divisive wars. The mission's recurring theme of teamwork also helped dispel the notion of the Army as a faceless, perhaps even soulless, top-down organization.

The media coverage was overwhelmingly supportive—with 94 percent of stories positive and the remaining 6 percent neutral, according to agency measurements. And the Creative Business Idea had the desired effect among young people: Enlistment went up by 1,000 soldiers, according to a report in the *Guardian*. Moreover, the minister of defense told the paper that 133,823 young people had "expressed an interest" in joining up, a 58 percent hike over the previous year. The Everest campaign delivered 40,000 target inquiries, a quarter of the Army's annual goal, in just two months.

Each stage
of the expedition
was turned into
a news story.

Sky News reached 98 million people with the reality drama.

"**Having Sky News embedded with the team made their daily reports more compelling.**"

—Holly Ward, Former Managing Director, Euro RSCG London PR

Regular radio diaries from the climbers were broadcast on 19 national and regional stations.

ON BRANDING IN THE DIGITAL AGE

"The Internet and social media have revolutionized the brand universe, making it a lot more complex, throwing brands in a sphere of cross-influence. On the one hand, brands have never faced such a threat of fragmentation—a threat of seeing the value and power of their brand diluted in this complex environment. On the other hand, they've never had such an opportunity to take the power of their brand to a great new dimension. Now they can turn their brand value into services, and thus redefine their role: publishing content, becoming a teacher, building communities... Statements are not enough; action is what is expected."

—Olivier Vigneaux, Managing Director, BETC Digital, in charge of strategy

"Digital changed everything—for our industry and for our agency. With our 'Digital at the Core' Creative Business Idea, we took the bold step of integrating the world's largest digital network, Euro RSCG 4D, into Euro RSCG, our main advertising and communications entity. This integration was not just in words, but philosophically, creatively, structurally, and financially. Our digital arm has been suffused throughout our company's body. And that is driving our clients' businesses and ours. 'Digital at the Core' will be our future... at least until we recognize that digital has changed everything again."

—George Gallate, Global Chairman, Euro RSCG 4D

"The underlying technology doesn't matter. The digital environment is about human relationships. If a brand knows how to behave and is able to create amazing assets in the digital world (destinations, rich content, entertainment, services, and more), it can make brilliant use of the social web. With a good amount of common sense, a brand can give the user tools to help proliferate its message. But be careful: By doing it in the wrong way, the collateral effects can be devastating. And by not doing anything, someone else (a consumer, for example) could drive it in the wrong direction. Whatever you do, make sure you do something and bring your specialists together."

—Wanessa Spiess, Chief Strategy Officer, Euro RSCG 4D Brazil

"Social media enables the free exchange of content and ideas among people, business, and brands, wherever you are. Come out of Farringdon tube station, check into Foursquare, and you'll find the best place for a latte—or, perhaps more important, the worst place, too. In this world you'd better have your house in order and something helpful, engaging, and of added value to contribute."

—Matt Atkinson, Former Global CEO, Euro RSCG 4D

ON BRANDING IN THE DIGITAL AGE

"The technological revolution has fragmented the audience and made it extremely difficult for brands to reach their targets. This has forced brands to interact, to engage further with their audiences, to deliver experience, to focus on building loyalty with their current customers—in other words, to produce a more valuable and involving content beyond what their products and messages were traditionally delivering."

—Christian de La Villehuchet, CEO, Euro RSCG Europe

"Digital/social media have significantly amplified the value and power of a brand name, for both good and ill. Brands that win the respect of their customers find themselves the subject of praise stamped with an imprimatur of customer-based authenticity. Brands that upset their customers can become subject to sustained attack on their reputation on multiple public fronts. As a result, brands have had to become highly responsive to customer sentiment—the ones that listen and respond win; the ones that ignore online comment do so at their own peril."

—Matt Ryan, Co-Chairman, Euro RSCG New York and President, Global Brands, Euro RSCG Worldwide

JAGUAR
"GORGEOUS"

CAN A CAR COMPANY REDEFINE LUXURY?

In 1961, Jaguar's E-Type was the marque of modern luxury—a true design and technology icon. With its long bonnet, chrome accents, leather interior, and top speed of 150 miles per hour, nothing else touched it. It was the ambassador for everything the brand stood for.

But something happened on the way to the next century. Jaguar's engines cooled, its pace slowed, and by 2005 the brand's once deafening roar had been reduced to a mewl. Jaguar was in the throes of a midlife crisis.

Gorgeous gets away with it.
PREFER GORGEOUS.COM

THE AGENCY OFFERED JAGUAR A BOLD YOUTH TONIC: STOP MAKING CAR ADS.

Poor kitty. For decades, Jaguar had been stalled in the gridlock of the overcrowded automotive category. U.S. sales alone were down 44 percent in 2004 over 2003. And the brand was wilting on a steady diet of German exhaust. BMW and Mercedes outspent Jaguar at every turn, touting German engineering and Autobahn speed. And then there was the growing threat from Japan in the shape of Lexus.

By comparison, the racing heart of Jaguar "sounded weak and felt old. It had become a brand that despite goodwill was ignored in the category," Daniel Floyed, global brand director at Euro RSCG Worldwide, told the client. The brand's 2001 grab for a younger crowd, the $30,000 X-Type, was criticized by the press and labeled an overpriced Ford. "Jaguar was a truly great luxury brand that had lost its way," Floyed says.

Euro RSCG's strategy was to position Jaguar as a new-fashioned luxury brand rather than as an automotive brand, giving it a place next to luxury icons such as Hermès, Tiffany, Louis Vuitton, and Chanel. The agency's "Gorgeous" campaign invited consumers to join Jaguar in a world that celebrated all things gorgeous. Its platinum-bathed solarized print and outdoor ads were a far cry from the category wallpaper of cars being shown going fast around corners.

High-end fashion photographer Michael Comte's two-week shoot produced enough stills and moving footage to sustain the brand's year-long relaunch and ongoing activities—all for 19 percent less than the previous year's production expenditure.

The integrated communications were more at home in *Vanity Fair* and *Vogue* than *Car and Driver*. Actor Willem Dafoe lent his distinctive gravelly voice to a brand film, purring lines such as "Gorgeous loves fast" and "Gorgeous gets in everywhere."

"There is a confidence luxury brands have. They have a steel backbone of unrivaled craftsmanship that never changes—all tempered with a relentless passion to innovate."
—Daniel Floyed, Global Brand Director, Euro RSCG Worldwide

"In choosing to be more than just a premium car brand, the management team had made a decision to be brave and walk the talk. They stood firm in order to realize the brand's potential—to allow Jaguar to be a new-fashioned luxury brand in its own right," Floyed says.

The audacious bet paid off. By the end of 2006, worldwide sales reached 13,307, up from 4,448 in 2005. "Gorgeous" had taken Jaguar from "poor kitty" to "kitty's got curves—and claws to match."

LUXURY AND
STYLE LEAD THE
MESSAGE AND
**TRANSFORM
JAGUAR
OVERNIGHT.**

An unbranded teaser campaign catches people off-guard. By communicating a clear point of view, Jaguar forces a reappraisal.

99%
sales increase in U.K. in first 6 weeks

100%
sales increase in U.S.

415%
sales increase in Germany

305%
sales increase worldwide in first year

Gorgeous gets in EVERYWHERE.

PREFERGORGEOUS.COM

French fashion designer Coco Chanel described luxury as the "absence of vulgarity," while American author and philosopher Henry David Thoreau decried it as a "hindrance to the elevation of mankind." Laud it or loathe it, the luxury market has been around almost as long as goods have been traded.

THE NEW LUXURY: MIND-SET OVER MONEY }

Granted, there has never been a single way to define luxury, nor a standard set of goods that qualify as such. At various times and places throughout history, such basics as sugar, soap, cotton, and chocolate have all been considered luxuries. What these items had in common were scarcity and prestige. They conveyed status upon those who used them not just because of their intrinsic benefits but also because they were available only to an elite few.

The modern luxury market would hardly be recognizable to earlier generations. Traditional luxuries (read: scarce and ultra-expensive) still exist, but the market has expanded considerably as affluence has increased and as luxury brands have extended their lines to include more widely available—and affordable—goods. What once was outside the purview of all but the upper echelons of society is now available to the majority in developed markets.

An equally significant change is that luxury is now largely self-defined so that it includes such things as a good night's sleep or a perfectly prepared cup of tea as well as many of the highest quality and scarcest goods. If it feels like a luxury to the owner/user, then it is a luxury.

What does this mean for marketers? Luxury is now less about price points than emotions, and value more often is judged as coming from the total experience of purchasing and owning the item rather than its market value. For some, a wool sweater hand-fashioned by a women's cooperative in an emerging market carries more value today than a sweater made of the finest cashmere but assembled anonymously in some luxury goods factory and for no greater purpose than being sold for a profit. Brand and product narratives—the stories about the people, processes, ingredients, and purpose behind the item—are essential; the more compelling the story, the more highly valued the product. In an increasingly artificial world, such elements as authentic provenance (Pipers Crisps made with "sea salt harvested from the Atlantic"), old-world techniques ("small-batch production," "hand-carved"), and connections to nature ("crafted from natural woods, reeds, bamboo, and grasses") have the capacity to elevate an everyday product into something truly special.

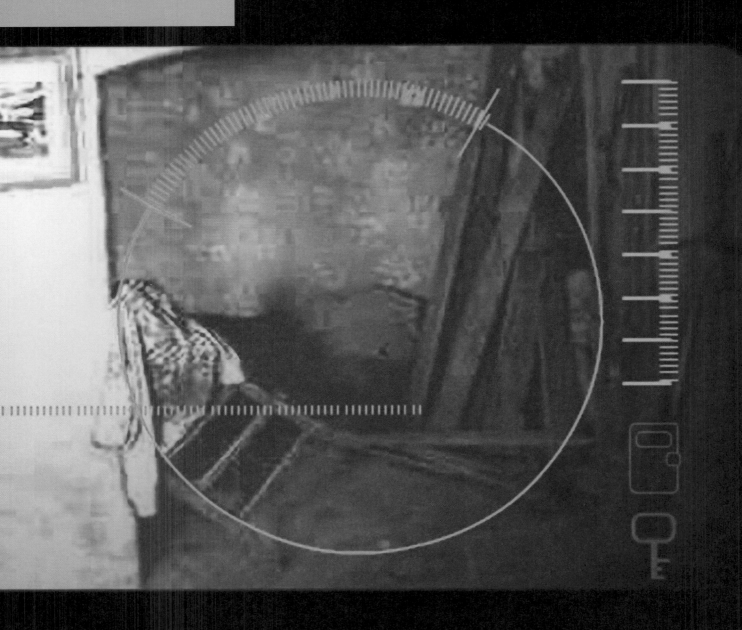

CAN A GAME BE A GAME-CHANGER?

In 1999, Nokia was the world's top mobile phone manufacturer, turning out handsets with the best battery life on the market. Its tagline, "Connecting People," made an emotional appeal, but its advertising efforts focused mainly on the products' technological edge. With competitors coming on fast, Nokia would have to make good on its promise to connect, and it would have to do it in a way that kept it ahead of the curve.

IS A BRAND THAT GENUINELY CONNECTS PEOPLE."

— Sicco Beerda, Former Executive Creative Director, Euro RSCG Netherlands

A future-focused company doesn't want to be held back by old ideas. The brand team at Euro RSCG in the Netherlands, headed by former executive creative director Sicco Beerda, tossed aside the notion of a traditional ad campaign in favor of a radically different approach: an alternate reality game—the first one ever created by an advertising agency. The Creative Business Idea was called simply "Nokia Game," and it was designed to build on social networking and user-generated content, which at the time were in their nascent stages of development on the Internet. "In the late nineties," says Beerda, "the Internet was a very different place. *Web 2.0* wasn't coined till years later, but already people were congregating in chat rooms and trying out new forms of engagement online. People were realizing they liked to play a more active role in their entertainment."

The agency knew it could create something entirely new by combining online and offline communications with Nokia's formidable technology. Unlike traditional storytelling, where audiences sit back and watch as the plot unfolds, Nokia Game would give consumers their own role, drawing them in with every clue and hurtling them through a real-world scavenger hunt propelled by clues sent via mobile phone and embedded in traditional media and online.

The plot line was formulaic but compelling: A young man named Sisu loses his memory after a snowboarding accident; it would be up to gamers to piece together his identity and the preceding events. The story aimed to draw in 15- to 35-year-old Europeans who were interested in technology but disenchanted with traditional advertising's hard sell.

Following a 1999 pilot program in the Netherlands, the adventure kicked off in 21 countries in 2000 with a TV ad directing viewers to a website. Driven by curiosity and a desire for something new, nearly half a million registered for the three-week program, despite not knowing exactly what it would be. The day before the game was to begin, participants received a cryptic phone message from one of the story's central characters: "I need your help."

A subsequent e-mail alerted players to an upcoming TV spot, which sent them to a website and then a newspaper. From there they raced to gather clues contained within SMS messages, TV movies, radio ads, voicemails, newspapers, anonymous phone calls, and more. Players who shared information moved through each round faster. Those who didn't advance at the required pace were eliminated. The first wave to solve the mystery was awarded Nokia's newest phone.

Players became engrossed in the game, establishing their own websites, trading tips, and positing theories. They held in-person meetings to exchange information and work out puzzles. By 2002, more than 1 million people in 25 countries were participating. "How's that for connecting people?" Beerda says. The game also created a strong baseline for the company, which continues to run interactive games.

Nokia Game changed the way consumers think about the brand. From a manufacturer of phone hardware, Nokia became an entertainment provider and connector. Long before the advent of smartphones and social networking, the game showed consumers how a piece of handheld technology could help shape their lives and create opportunities for socialization. The effort earned the agency a Gold Lion Direct Award at the International Advertising Festival in Cannes in 2002.

The game also launched a marketing genre. Since Nokia Game, marketers have used alternate reality games to promote such things as Audi automobiles, *Halo 2*, Steven Spielberg's film *A.I. Artificial Intelligence*, and the ABC series *Lost*, all to great effect. Nokia showed that creating a compelling story and an intriguing interactive platform builds connections between people—and between people and brands.

A DEDICATED COMMUNITY SPANS 25 COUNTRIES—
AND A NEW MARKETING GENRE IS LAUNCHED.

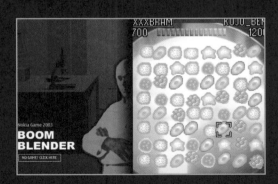

Digital is massive, and with so many brilliant minds focused on the space we can be certain that someone will come along who changes things more radically than any of the rest of us anticipated. The digital world of today looks very different from how it will look in just a few years, but there are certain fundamental truths that will continue to have an impact on marketing communications.

FOUR TRUTHS ABOUT OUR DIGITAL FUTURE

Fernanda Romano, Global Creative Director, Digital and Experiential, Euro RSCG Worldwide

1.
Digital will force us to become better storytellers

Consumers are spending more and more time connected to the Internet from a multitude of devices, so this is where we will have to go in order to connect with them. That means we will need to get even better at storytelling, so they will *want* to spend time with us. We've come a very long way from those first awfully limited brand websites, those first banner ads, partly because we are better integrated now; there is no longer a physical or psychological space between traditional and digital advertising.

One of the ways we'll continue to improve our storytelling is by getting better at designing games, which really are just a form of nonlinear tale-spinning. Before long, new technologies will make games even more engaging, involving not just the click of a finger but whole body movement. We will be able to invite people into virtual worlds that will make our current technologies seem stale and flat. And we will be able to create social media environments with multiple narrators weaving ongoing stories in collaboration with players.

2.

Location will be the place to be

From an advertising and storytelling perspective, location will become a bigger part of the picture. We're focusing more on where we are gathered online, paying more attention to the fact that both of us are on Facebook, say, rather than one being physically in London and the other in Tokyo, but most of our mobile devices are capable of tagging our physical locations. The next generation will feature greater awareness of physical proximity—and when that happens, the story lines will change as well. With both spaces to play in, we will have twice the opportunities to interact and engage. And there will be no more difference between our existence in cyberspace and real space.

3.

Consumers will control our content

No matter how prolific we are as copywriters or art directors, we will always be grossly outnumbered, and our messages increasingly will have to compete with those generated by others working and playing in the same digital space. If we're smart about it,

we will find new and more creative ways to collaborate—for starters, by keeping in mind that whatever we put out there will remain there in perpetuity, to be acted upon and repurposed as people see fit. It will be to our advantage to create content people want to engage with and play with and make their own. Our stories are no longer ours to control.

4.

We'll get better at mobile conversations

Amid all the gadgets out there, one device has become the modern consumer's lifeline: the cell phone. And we haven't even scratched the surface of what these phones are capable of. Mobile computing is something communications companies should be all over, because the smartphone is not a phone; it is a computer—a computer that will plug us into the cloud that will allow us to collaborate, to create and receive content, to be part of the conversation. Only by understanding how mobile computing is working right now and where it is going next can we play the game.

RATP
"MOBILITY
PROVIDER"

CAN MASS TRANSIT BE A LIFESTYLE BRAND?

Overcrowded. Dirty. Dangerous. Déclassé. That's how people described the Paris Métro in the 1990s. How did RATP, the Paris subway and bus transportation system, want people to think of it? As economical, fast, and ecology-minded. So it asked BETC Euro RSCG to create an ad campaign that would improve the system's image. The agency said no.

For the system to successfully transform its image, riders would have to more than tolerate the Métro. They would have to enjoy using it.

BETC Euro RSCG knew advertising wasn't going to solve RATP's problems. Overhauling the troubled brand's image would require a massive injection of positive word of mouth, and that meant it would have to re-create the experience of the metro system's diverse ridership—young and old, students and businesspeople, rich and poor. And it especially needed to wow those customers the agency called "advanced consumers living mobile lives"—passengers aged 20 to 40 who relied on the Métro not just to commute to and from work but even more so for shopping, entertainment, meeting friends, and escaping.

Euro RSCG was determined to make RATP more than a transportation company. It would become a service company that was in the business of making people more mobile. Digital signs announcing train arrival times were installed in all subway stations, as were automatic ticket machines to better serve younger passengers accustomed to do-it-yourself online purchasing. Contact-free electronic passes were made available, and RATP began partnering with bike rental company Vélib to allow patrons to use the same card to ride the subway or a bicycle. To encourage customers to hop aboard more often, RATP launched *A Nous Paris*, a weekly entertainment guide detailing events around the city.

The Paris Métro became a destination in itself. Stations were redesigned to be more comfortable and pleasing. Numerous entrances were transformed into works of art. The stop at Saint-Germain, for example, near where literary greats Jean-Paul Sartre, Simone de Beauvoir, and Ernest Hemingway once convened, was redesigned around the theme of poetry and literature; the Arts et Métiers station, below the Conservatory of Arts and Crafts, resembles the inside of a submarine. In a number of stations, RATP also added shops and vending kiosks, meeting spaces, and galleries, where performances could be held. Cultural partnerships with music festivals and others were forged, with commemorative RATP tickets available for special events.

In the year following RATP's redirection as a "mobility provider," traffic rose to a record-high 2.64 billion trips, and the number of annual passes sold hit 750,000 (up from 150,000 in 1995). More than 300 subway stations were renovated, refurbished with new lights, seating, and flooring. The RATP website has come to include interactive maps and live timetables. Most important, riding the Métro has become a preferred option, perfect for mobile Parisians zipping to their next diversion, rather than a commuter's drudgery.

**19 h 15 : Notre-Dame,
20 h : Parc des Princes.**

RATP

*LA MEILLEURE
FAÇON D'AVANCER.*

STRIKING NEW STATION GRAPHICS MAKE FOR HAPPIER RIDERS.

**13 h : Puces de St-Ouen,
13 h 45 : Zoo de Vincennes.**

RATP

*LA MEILLEURE
FAÇON D'AVANCER.*

BEYOND WORDS

It's not just brands that need to adapt and change and think beyond traditional industry boxes; agencies, too, must constantly move into new arenas to ensure they have the knowledge and tools to open up important new opportunities for clients. With its acquisition of a majority stake in THE:HOURS in 2008, Euro RSCG Worldwide became the first major advertising network to own a record label.

By adding a music consultancy group to the agency roster, Euro RSCG is able to take full advantage of opportunities for artistic collaboration around the world.

Traditionally, advertisers have focused their branding efforts on visuals and text—on the work of art directors and copywriters. Now, with consumers not connecting as much with the traditional marketing mix (TV commercials, print ads, radio, outdoor), music, scent, touch, and other elements that stimulate the senses in creative and original ways are more critical. THE:HOURS partnership offers Euro RSCG and its clients instant access to the specialized knowledge, approaches, and tools of the music industry. A few examples of how the new tool has been used:

For luxury brand Cartier's "Love" campaign, THE:HOURS commissioned songs by a dozen hand-picked artists in key global markets, including Lou Reed, Marion Cotillard, Dan Black, and Phoenix. The songs were made available exclusively for streaming and downloading on Cartier's Love website. Sales of the Love collection increased 20 percent during the promotion.

For Tommy Hilfiger's new fragrance master brand Loud, THE:HOURS brought British rock duo The Ting Tings into the action even before the fragrance was created. The Ting Tings provided input on the scent as it was being formulated and refined and then wrote and recorded an original song, "We're Not the Same," to give the fragrance a strong vibe and sensibility, and connect it with its millennial generation target.

For the "TckTckTck" environmental campaign (see pages 271–277), the label asked Peter Garnett, lead vocalist for the rock band Midnight Oil (before becoming Australia's minister of the environment), to rewrite the band's hit song "Beds Are Burning" to address the topic of climate change. THE:HOURS then worked with a broad array of international music stars and celebrities—from Fergie and Duran Duran to Youssou N'Dour and Mark Ronson—to record the new track. To minimize costs and carbon footprint, the video

of the song was filmed in various parts of the world. THE:HOURS then used the assembled piece to launch a music video that would become the first-ever digital music petition: Anyone in the world could visit the TckTckTck site as well as dozens of online music stores such as iTunes and become a "climate ally" by downloading the song. Fifteen million people did so in advance of the climate summit in Copenhagen in 2009.

In 2010, THE:HOURS teamed with Goom Radio to launch the first-ever HD digital radio service for an advertising agency, Euro RSCG. THE:HOURS Radio broadcasts the agency's culture and sound to listeners via Internet radio, free of charge. The content includes a mix of rock, pop, and electronic music, plus radio shows, deejay mixes, interviews, and live concerts, all of which can be embedded and shared across social networks.

"THE:HOURS illustrates how the music and advertising industries are increasingly rubbing shoulders," says Alexandre Sap, president and CEO of THE:HOURS. "With this partnership, we are able to work with Euro RSCG to develop new business models and generate new sources of revenue and exposure for clients. It's the sort of profitable collaboration we'll see more of as brands work harder to create an indelible impression on their audiences."

TARGETING THE NEW CONSUMER

WE'RE LIVING IN AN ERA of unparalleled change, and nowhere is this more evident than in the arena of consumerism. As shoppers, we have all been empowered with new tools (price-comparison engines, e-coupons), new means of communication and collaboration (group buying, peer reviews), and more informed and equitable relationships with brands and their parent companies. We now have 24/7 access to customer service, can learn just about anything we want about a company online, and have myriad ways (from a simple chat room post to a YouTube exposé) to express our feelings about businesses and brands.

Standing out among these more-empowered consumers is a subset of shoppers Euro RSCG Worldwide has been tracking for more than a decade, a demographic segment that is influencing—and even driving—markets across the globe. We call these men and women *Prosumers*, originally as a nod to their role as **pro***active* con**sumers**, and over the years we have devoted substantial resources to monitoring their evolution in the face of the massive changes society has undergone, from the world's radical technological revolution to globalization, from business scandals and financial crises to terrorism, health threats, and our burgeoning eco-consciousness.

Key Traits: Prosumers...

- Embrace innovation, are curious to try new things, challenges, and experiences.
- Are keen on new technology and gadgets.
- Transport new attitudes, ideas, and behavior—they are "human media."
- Recognize their value as consumers and expect brand partners to do likewise.
- Are marketing-savvy and plugged in to multiple media sources.
- Demand top-notch customer service and access to information.
- Proactively seek to maximize control over their lives through information, communication, and technology.
- Constantly seek information and opinions; are eager to share their views and experiences with others.

In their earliest iteration, Prosumers stood out from the mainstream because of their insatiable desire for information, for new products and experiences, and for the bragging rights that come from being in the know ahead of the rest. They were also far more brand-aware than average, cognizant of their worth as consumers, and insistent on being respected and catered to by their brand partners. They were more apt than others, for instance, to expect something (a discount or more personalized service, perhaps) in exchange for giving information to a company. As early and enthusiastic adopters of new technologies, they were well ahead of the curve in getting online and figuring out how to use the newly available access to information and communications to best advantage. These were the first people out there comparing prices on Shopzilla, reading and posting product reviews on Epinions, and loudly making known any complaints they might have about a product, a company, or a brand experience on message boards and in consumer forums.

In the years since, Prosumers continued to grow as proactive consumers, but they also became **pro**_ducer_ con**sumers** (in keeping with the origins of the term coined by futurologist Alvin Toffler in his 1980 best seller _The Third Wave_), generating their own content and taking hold of whatever spheres of influence and creativity caught their fancies online. They customized brand offerings through such sites as NIKEiD and applied themselves to filling in any perceived gaps in the brand universe—bypassing traditional retailers by bidding on eBay or bartering on Craigslist, building their own computer and phone "apps" (or mixing and matching those created by others), and finding ever more inventive ways to improve the fit and function of their personal worlds. So, too, did they become **pro***fessional* con**sumers**, pursuing their passions in areas such as audio, video, photography, cooking, and DIY with the sorts of high-end tools and equipment (La Cornue stoves, DSLR cameras) that once were exclusive to professionals in the field. From their decked-out kitchens and spa bathrooms to their home workshops and media rooms, Prosumers began to blur the line between amateurism and professionalism.

Now we're seeing yet another iteration of Prosumerism, as these influencers move into the realm of **pro***gressive* con**sumers**, using their spending as an activist tool. These shoppers are now far more conscious—and conscientious— about the choices they make as consumers and the effect their consumption is having on other people and the planet. They are rejecting the heedless excess of past decades in favor of something more satisfying and sustainable. They are the people who are "buying local" to support their communities and feel more connected to producers. They are paying attention to their carbon footprints and prefer to buy products that are organic, Fair Trade, cause-related, or the like.

More than a decade into our studies, Prosumers have grown more powerful, more proactive, and more passionate. Around the globe, these people are changing the rules of brand interaction. To a large extent, they are calling the shots when it comes to their relationships with brands, but that's only part of the story. Thanks to new means of communication—social media, in particular—brands have an opportunity to engage them in more meaningful and enduring ways. As marketers, it is up to us to work alongside them, involving them in our work, learning from them, and, at times, even ceding some measure of control to them.

In this chapter, we look at some of the innovative ways in which we have worked with clients to communicate with today's more empowered and demanding consumers, satisfying their desires for direct dialogue, a more substantive way of living, and a more engaging brand experience. These cases cover a broad spectrum of industries, ranging from telephony to fast food to publishing.

"If digitally empowered Prosumers don't like what you are doing, they may well decide to take your company and your brand down."

—David Jones, Global CEO, Havas and Euro RSCG Worldwide

THE PREDICTAMETER

Proving the
Validity of
Euro RSCG's
Prosumer Tool

We can predict the future using our Prosumer tool. Yes, and the moon is made of cheese.

That was often the kind of conversation Euro RSCG India would have with clients. Companies were tired of agencies boasting about their strategic processes and thought ours was yet another audacious claim with little or no substance.

We needed a way to prove that our tool did have predictive ability. Yet we couldn't risk sharing the confidential data of one client with another. So what sort of test case could we use? What could we expose Prosumers to and then track how well their "likes" and "dislikes" translated into market results? How could we prove that Prosumers really do drive markets? In the end, we chose one of the most difficult categories to predict—but also the one guaranteed to give us greatest buzz: the box-office success of Bollywood movies. We made a list of 32 yet-to-be-released Hindi films and predicted which ones would succeed and which would not based on feedback from Prosumers. All the movies were slated for release over three months, giving us a compact test period.

Our methodology was simple: We made a concept card for each of the movies based on publicly available information about them. Then we conducted quantitative research in four cities. The questionnaire included Euro RSCG's Prosumer algorithm so we could identify the Prosumers in each sample; it asked respondents to predict the success of each upcoming movie on a five-point scale from super hit to super flop. We then created a weighted average of the results, giving a much higher weight to Prosumers than to main-stream respondents.

From leading popular print publications to trade media and news channels, the media were all over the story. We created quite a controversy, with many filmmakers denouncing our claims as preposterous since we were predicting—based on the views of our Prosumers—that some big-budget movies with famous superstars were going to flop. Then we tracked how each of the rated films actually did. We conducted the experiment for two years running: In the first year we achieved an 80 percent success rate, while in the second year we got more than 90 percent right. Naturally, we crowed about this in the media as well as in credentials presentations to clients. Many of our clients and prospects had followed the story in the media and already knew the case study before we presented it.

That was our greatest reward. Well, that and being able to prove what we had long known our Prosumer tool could do.

ON THE NEW CONSUMER

"Up until recently, traditional media were the main vehicle with which to attract potential customers. It was mainly one-way communication. Now the wired consumer is keen to engage with the brand and other consumers, through social media, before he decides to espouse a brand or a product. He wants the brand to be a statement about his personality, his beliefs, and the social group with which he affiliates himself."

—Pierre Soued, Managing Director, Euro RSCG Middle East

"THE NEW CONSUMER EXPECTS TWO-WAY, OPEN, AND ENGAGING CONVERSATIONS. FOR THAT REASON, THEY POSE A CHALLENGE TO BIG BRANDS THAT HAVE A FORMULAIC WAY OF PUSHING MESSAGES TO CUSTOMERS. BRANDS THAT CAN ENGAGE AND BE TRANSPARENT AND NOT OBSESS ABOUT BEING IN CONTROL WILL PROSPER."

—Matt Fanshawe, Managing Director, Euro RSCG Asia Pacific

"You're only as good as your business is, does, and delivers. In the old world you could probably get away with an average business (and God knows there are still some around), but your brand is increasingly not what you say and do, but what others say and do. It brings me back to one of my favorite ways of talking about a brand: A great brand is defined by what people say about you when you aren't there."

— Matt Atkinson, Former Global CEO, Euro RSCG 4D

"First, consumers spoke about products; now they talk about brands. They want the brand to be in the product; they want to know more about its history, the way it was made, about the heart that went into it. Even more striking, behind these brands they see a company and the values put into it by the people who work there."

—Mercedes Erra, Executive President, Euro RSCG Worldwide, President, Euro RSCG France, Managing Director, Havas, and Founder, BETC Euro RSCG

COCA-COLA
"PATH TO
PURCHASE"

HOW DO YOU REEL THEM IN AT RETAIL?

Underdog is not a term one generally associates with Coca-Cola. The iconic brand is blessed with big ad budgets, near-universal brand awareness, and a global distribution network second to none. But in Southeast Asia in 2007, Coke was being stung by a raft of small brands with the home-field advantage.

COKE WAS NO STRANGER TO THE region, having been there since the 1970s, but it had yet to upset the local favorites. Sales were declining even as brands with virtually no advertising were going strong. Traditional tea and milk drinks such as Pokka, Yeo's Chrysanthemum Tea, and Milo were convenience store kings. After all those years, Coke was still a challenger.

"Coke would create heaps of brand love, but they weren't converting that into sales," says Matt Fanshawe, managing director of Euro RSCG Asia Pacific. "People would see a Coke ad on TV, but then they'd get into the store and walk out with another brand."

Coca-Cola, a master of mass communication, was ending the conversation too soon—after its campaigns had captured imaginations but before sealing the deal with shoppers. That gave local brands the chance to jump in. Euro RSCG Singapore decided it was time to get personal.

Now-ubiquitous brand clutter has made it easy for consumers to tune out marketing come-ons; it takes something special to get their attention. As part of Euro RSCG's strategy for Coke, the agency identified four zones in which the brand could chat up its customers. Together they mirror a shopper's usual path through a store, as well as his thoughts in real time. At the first zone, outside a local 7-11 test store, parched passersby might see a winking billboard, Pop Art signs, and bus shelter ads tempting consumers—particularly teenagers— inside for a cold one. The art featured an open Coke bottle with effervescent bubbles and stars

escaping from the top. Copy offered a flirty invitation, engaging consumers directly with a simple "Hello" or "Drink me." "We wanted to introduce the occasion to them: Three o'clock, after school, is the perfect time for a Coke," says Leonardo O'Grady, director of sparkling activation platforms for Coca-Cola Pacific Group.

"PATH TO PURCHASE" SPARKED A CONVERSATION THAT TOOK SHOPPERS FROM SIDEWALK TO CASH REGISTER, GROOVY RED CAN IN HAND.

At the transition zone—the store's sliding glass door and floors—decals pointed the way toward a frosty Coke. The impulse zone—the magazine and snack aisles—offered coupons and reinforced Coke's come-on with signs that said, "I'm that way" or offered 20-cent savings to "Snack with me." And at the destination zone, Coke installed coolers wrapped with campaign images and price-point decals. The bottles featured hang tags with copy like "Choose me" or "99 cents of pure joy."

A quarter of shoppers said the signs moved them to buy a Coca-Cola drink; brand sales increased 17 percent. A packaging redesign, which brought the can in line with the campaign's cheeky tone, earned creative kudos at the 2009 Spikes Asia Awards.

Singapore's success turned the brand's top-down marketing program on its head. The "Path to Purchase" became "The Coke Way of Retail," the definitive retail bible for Coca-Cola worldwide.

RESULTS:
17% SALES HIKE

Euro RSCG and Coke created a "retail bible" that integrated signage, package design, and event promotion. It became the blueprint for Coke point-of-sale promotions worldwide.

ON THE NEW CONSUMER

"We're living in a world where it's all about collaboration rather than control. We used to police our brands and be absolutely obsessive about controlling everything. Today it is much more important to create content that people want to pass around and share than it is to actually retain control and ownership. We're no longer living in a linear world; we live in a square world where, if your message and content and brand are sufficiently engaging and interesting for consumers, they will take it upon them-selves to help build your brand."

—David Jones, Global CEO, Havas and Euro RSCG Worldwide

"We are living the most important information revolution the world has known since the Gutenberg press. TV was nothing compared to the way technology has empowered consumers. Our clients who have relied for a long time on a command-and-control paradigm must understand they no longer own their brands. Consumers are in the pilot's seat. Brands that don't realize that conversation and transparency, honesty and sincerity, are the new paradigm will die. Only the brands that delegate power and control to consumers will make it to the future."

—François de Rivière, Creative Strategy Director, Euro RSCG Southeast Asia

"The keyboard is now the tool of choice for consumers who wish to voice their opinions. They can use it to tear down brands in a worldwide virtual storm of negativity in days or to enshrine the brand in love and praise for the world to see forever. The reach of opinions and conversations is no longer limited to your immediate circle of friends. And 'word of mouse' doesn't dissipate like a verbal conversation; it lives in pixel perpetuity well after the campaign or brand was experienced. If you have a consistently and distinctively positioned brand, substantiated by great product and service delivery, then you will be loved and talked about, creating a virtuous cycle of positivity and building a powerful brand legacy."

—Daniel Lee, Regional Digital Director, Euro RSCG Southeast Asia

CAN JESUS SAVE HOLLYWOOD?

CAN YOU RETHINK THINKING?

"When did we stop thinking?" It's not often an ad campaign fathoms the big questions, but for *The Atlantic* magazine, Euro RSCG New York did nothing but. The agency's effort to reinvigorate the brand invited readers to "Think. Again" by building a campaign around the publication's own puzzlers.

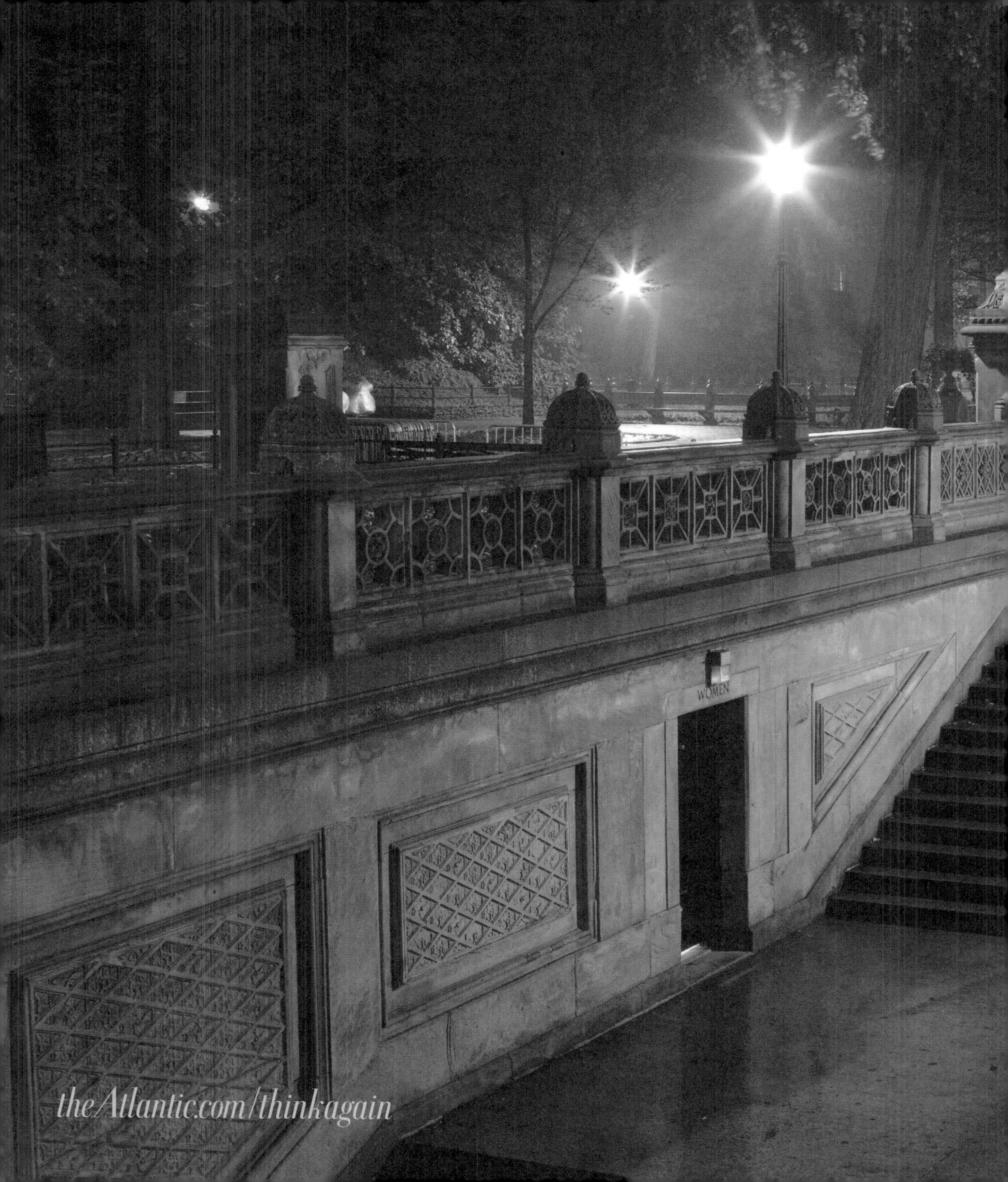
WOMEN
theAtlantic.com/thinkagain

WHEN IS EVIL COOL?

the *Atlantic*
Think. Again.

WHY DO
PRETEND

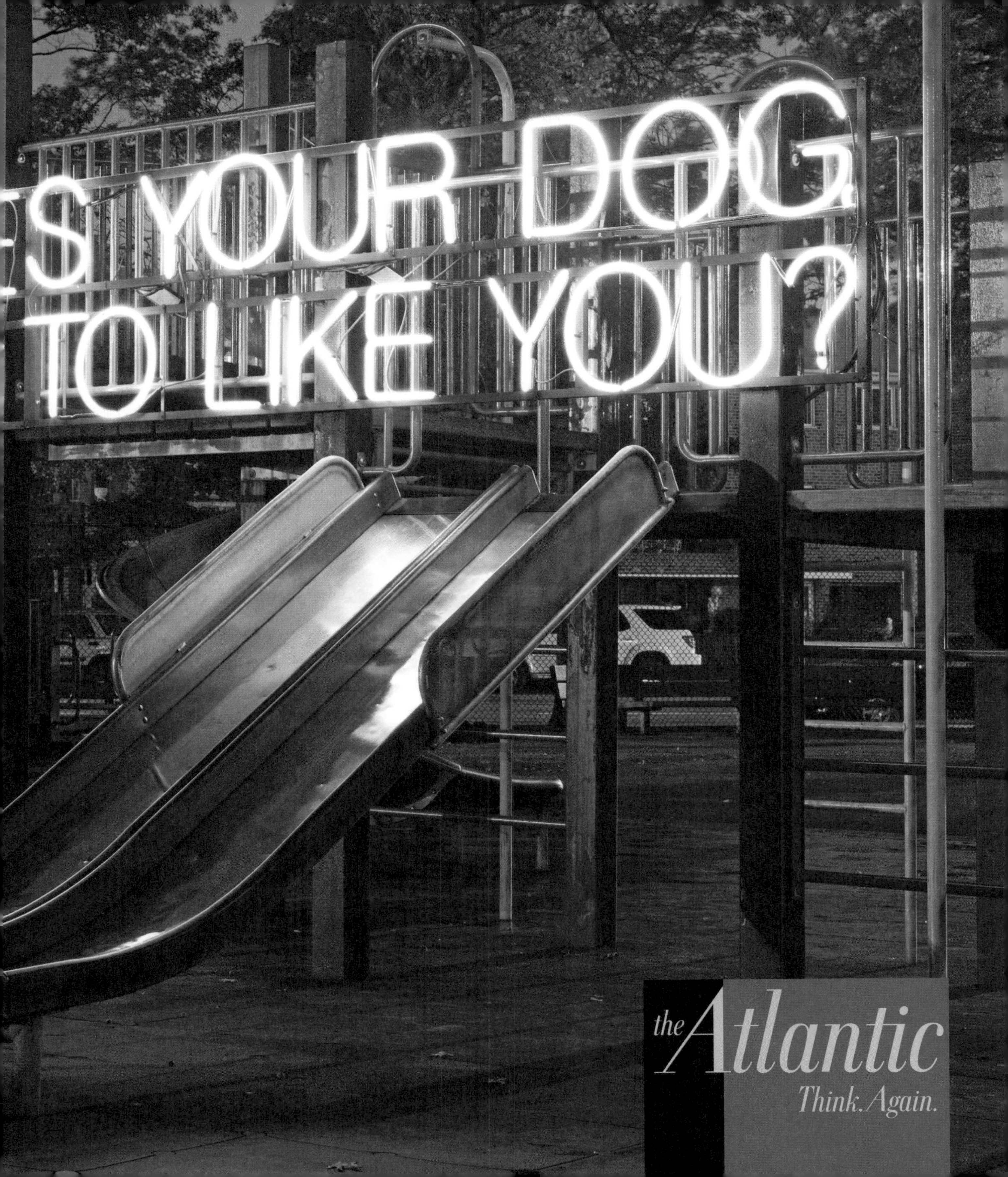
S YOUR DOG
TO LIKE YOU?
the Atlantic
Think. Again.

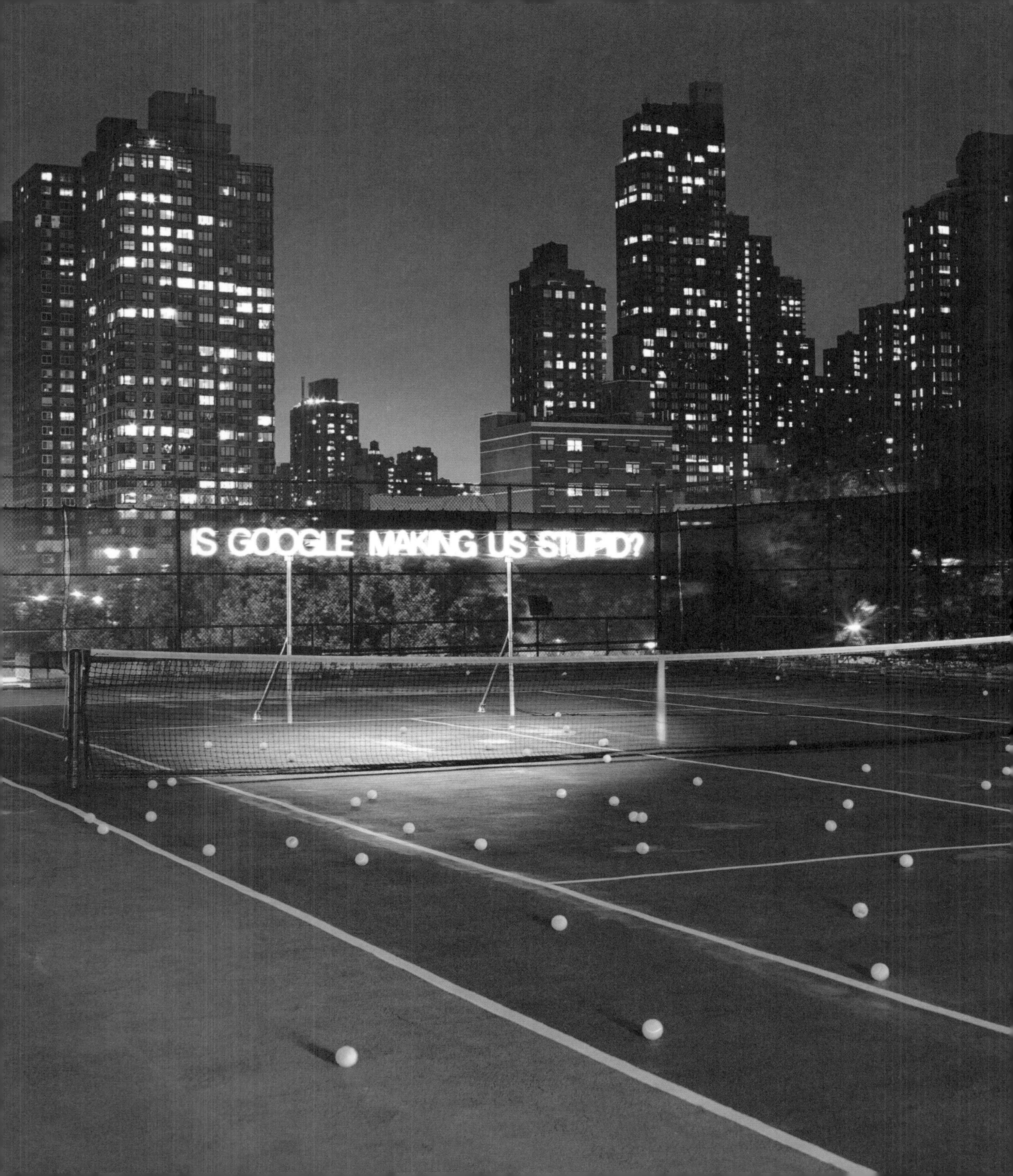
IS GOOGLE MAKING US STUPID?

SEVEN IN TEN.

That's how many people think we're all turning into bubbleheads, according to a recent survey. Specifically, they worry that society has become too shallow, that we spend too much time thinking about things that don't really matter. Not great news for any brand that relies on an audience of critical thinkers. Such was the challenge facing *The Atlantic*, a venerated American magazine for 150 years but one whose advertising base and circulation were stagnant. Would this celebrated publication, founded by the likes of Emerson, Longfellow, and Oliver Wendell Holmes, Sr., fall victim to short-burst texting and reality TV?

"Reading *The Atlantic* was seen as a hard slog. Homework. Intellectual heavy lifting," says Andrew Benett, global CEO of Arnold Worldwide and chief strategy officer of Havas Worldwide. "*The New Yorker* made readers feel hip and *The Economist* made them feel well-informed. Readers were worried *The Atlantic* would make them feel intellectually wiped out."

The magazine turned to Euro RSCG to find a way to remind people of how wonderful an experience it is to think. The agency knew thinkers were out there, hungry for a real meal after a steady diet of low-nutrition brain snacks.

Rather than seeking out the tweedy academic types who had long been associated with the publication, the agency went looking for the young, fiery thinkers who make up the New Intelligentsia—men and women running tech start-ups, acquiring patents, pushing through change. To sell this target audience on *The Atlantic*, the agency issued invitations to "Think. Again" in the form of provocative questions posted in public places. A passerby might find "Is war a sport?" posted on a muffin top, "Does oil have a future?" on a sandwich board, "Is God an accident?" affixed to a display of suntan lotions. In addition, Euro RSCG's crews planted 14 oversized neon questions, all drawn from *The Atlantic*'s own editorial pages, in key locations around New York City, then filmed people's answers on the spot and posted the videos to the magazine's website. "Is the donut doomed?" asked one sign. "As long as there is a cop around, the donut will not be doomed," quipped a bystander. "Is America still the land of opportunity?" Responded one passerby, "You cannot be American born, because you're not going to make it. Too complacent. You gotta be immigrant."

"We wanted to catch people when they weren't thinking. The whole idea was to get their prefrontal cortexes firing again."

—Andrew Benett, Global CEO, Arnold Worldwide and Chief Strategy Officer, Havas Worldwide

The resulting videos, posted on the microsite thinkagain.theatlantic.com, were viewed in 139 countries, increasing traffic on the site 51 percent and extending the campaign's impact far beyond New York. Equally important, in addition to readers and subscribers, a new breed of modern, consumer-driven advertisers, including Apple, Audi, and Paramount Vantage, was drawn to the magazine. Digital revenue spiked 197 percent against the same period the year prior. And the first print issue that closed following the launch of The Atlantic Project outpaced its predecessor by 35 percent. Oh, yes— and the total ad budget was just $300,000. Viral and print make fine bedfellows after all.

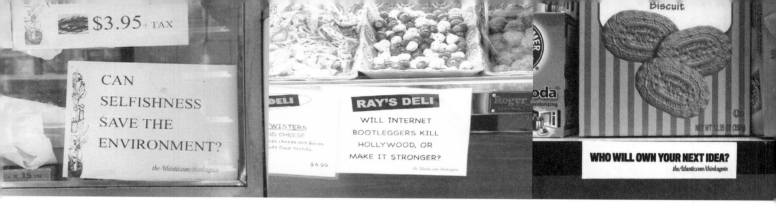

WILD POSTINGS MOVED THE CONVERSATION
INTO UNLIKELY LOCATIONS,
CATCHING READERS OFF-GUARD.

LIVE INTERVIEWS CAPTURED CANDID REACTIONS
FROM PASSERSBY TO THE AMBIENT CAMPAIGN
AND FUELED THE DEBATE ON THE WEBSITE.

THE CAMPAIGN EVEN
TRANSLATED TO
THE MAGAZINE'S FRONT
COVER.

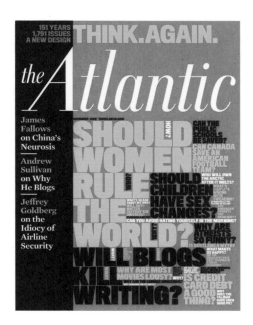

MICROSITE VIEWED IN 139 COUNTRIES

TRAFFIC TO WEB INCREASED 51%

DIGITAL REVENUE UP 197%

FIRST POST-LAUNCH ISSUE UP 35%

CAN YOU REINVENT THE PHONE COMPANY?

Hutchison Telecommunications was building a wireless phone network in Australia. The problem? With four competing networks already in place, the market was saturated. Worse yet, research showed that Aussies were frustrated by the mobile-telephone category. They found juggling their existing phones overly complicated and didn't want to add yet another service to their telecom mix. Euro RSCG Sydney's solution? Invent an entirely new category: a new kind of phone that lets consumers simplify their lives by using a single service for home and away.

Soon home phones will go mobile.

Call 133 488

the future's bright, the future's Orange

orange™

hutchison telecoms

THE NEW TECHNOLOGY ENABLED CUSTOMERS TO DROP THEIR LANDLINES SO THEY WOULD NO LONGER HAVE TO JUGGLE TWO PHONE NUMBERS, TWO VOICEMAIL ACCOUNTS, TWO TELEPHONES.

Orange One.

Now home phones can go mobile.

call 133 488

the future's bright, the future's orange.

orange™

hutchison telecoms

Orange One. Now sharing a house doesn't mean sharing a phone.

Call 133 488
the future's bright, the future's Orange

orange
hutchison telecoms

HUTCHISON HAD AN ADVANTAGE over its rivals: Its network was built on a triangular configuration of base stations, which enabled it to identify whether a call was placed from home. That meant it could charge different rates: lower for calls made at home, higher for calls made on the go. More significant, this technology would free customers from their landline phones, meaning they would no longer have to juggle two phone numbers, two voicemail accounts, two telephones. They would be able to take only one phone with them anywhere they went. And there was another advantage: In 2000, only 30 percent of Internet users in Australia had a dedicated phone line for online service, and there were long waits to obtain one from the market leader. With its new all-in-one phone, Orange freed up the existing home phone line for Internet use.

The client-agency team called the product Orange One—one phone, one line rental, one bill—to convey its simplicity. The question was how to get the word out in a cost-effective way. The team opted for a two-pronged approach. In its traditional advertising, Euro RSCG Sydney broke free from category restrictions, replacing the usual scenes of people chattering away on sidewalks and in shopping malls with a symbol: an orange hot-air balloon that represented the freedom of movement and flexibility

Orange One conferred. Tethered to a base, the balloon stood for calls from home; untethered, it represented calls made on the move. The icon was simple, bright, and cheerful, and it appeared everywhere. In addition to the balloon images on print and outdoor ads and direct marketing pieces, real balloons hovered over community and sporting events to signal Orange One's sponsorship. Brand awareness in Sydney and Melbourne skyrocketed to 82 percent.

In another break from category conventions, the team deployed a squadron of balloon-emblazoned vans driven by door-to-door salesmen—the old-school method used in previous eras by vacuum and encyclopedia companies. While competitors held to retail locations, Orange One demonstrated its flexibility and convenience by bringing the service directly to customers' homes.

Online, e-mail blasts were sent to household decision makers, particularly those in homes with a single line juggling voice and Internet services. Those e-mails reinforced the idea that customers could surf the Internet and talk on the phone at the same time if they subscribed to Orange One. After just four months on the market, Orange One racked up 76,500 customers.

With a breakthrough creative idea and a simple sales pitch, Euro RSCG Sydney turned a complicated technology into a household helper by recognizing that what Orange One was selling was not just a phone service but a FREEDOM SERVICE.

MCDONALD'S

"COME AS
YOU ARE"

CAN YOU SELL FAST FOOD ON AMBIENCE?

When McDonald's debuted in France in the 1970s, Gallic gastronomes made much ado about the incursion of the American restaurant chain and its quick, cheap food. Two all-beef patties, special sauce, lettuce, cheese, pickles, onions on a sesame seed bun was a recipe some weren't prepared to swallow.

"McDonald's was perceived as American food that attacked our deep culture of cooking," says Clarisse Lacarrau, associate planning director at BETC Euro RSCG in Paris. And its casual service culture was offensive. In France, diners are acutely aware of the rules of dining decorum: Proper attire and good manners are required, and a social stratum applies. "It's not a laid-back country when it comes to food and restaurants," she says.

come
as you
are. M

WHATEVER YOUR WALK OF LIFE, YOU'RE WELCOME AT MCDONALD'S.

come as you are.

In time, the chain lured French eaters into its restaurants with better interiors, local ingredients, and more sophisticated menu items (ciabatta buns instead of sesame seed; authentic mustard in place of standard American yellow). By 2006, there were more than 1,000 McDonald's restaurants in France, and a year later the country had become the fast-food chain's second most profitable market after the U.S.

But it had also become a victim of its own success. Once the subject of a fierce national debate, the brand had long since been accepted with a shrug. "At this time, McDonald's was perceived as a provider of practical food," Lacarrau says. "It wasn't hated or loved. It was just functional." Campaigns touted its convenience and quick service, but that tactic had grown stale. After years of growth, sales had gone flat, and the primary core values—passion and love—weren't there anymore.

The team at BETC Euro RSCG knew they needed to reignite French passions, to get people thinking about why they enjoy McDonald's over the many other dining options available to them. And they hit upon an idea: Rather than play up the brand's local touches, they would stay true to its relaxed American roots. They would show the restaurant as a warm, welcoming place, free from the social norms that dictate who dines where. Using the tagline "Come as you are," the 2008 print and TV campaign positioned McDonald's as an antidote to France's fastidious dining culture.

Early print ads reinforced the concept with a series of photographs of a single model styled as a businessperson, hippie, beach bum, and exerciser in workout gear. In 2009, ads featured Darth Vader comfortably munching on a burger, presumably taking a break from the pressures of running The Empire. In another, King Kong retrieves his takeout without anyone calling in air support.

Later TV ads offered backup to the "Come as you are" tagline. In "Father and Son," a young gay man's sexuality is revealed to the audience even as his father, seated across the table, remains oblivious. Other ads show a turning point in a mother-daughter squabble and a pair of oldsters masquerading in an online chat room as a supermodel and surfer. Such shenanigans might be frowned upon at fussier dining establishments, but at McDonald's patrons are never judged.

The campaign resonated with French consumers. At the end of the first year, 63 percent of those polled were aware of the new tagline, 70 percent liked the campaign, and 89 percent remembered it accurately as a McDonald's campaign. Meanwhile, the chain's growth received a welcome boost: up 7.9 percent year over year in 2008, the biggest hike in all European markets.

"McDonald's is really the restaurant for everybody," Lacarrau says. "People can feel free to be themselves. They don't have to worry about the way they talk and dress and eat."

ON DIGITAL YOUTH

"OLD MARKETING RECIPES AND OLD RESEARCH TOOLS DO NOT WORK FOR THE DIGITAL GENERATION, BUT TODAY'S YOUTH CAN REALLY FUNCTION AS STRONG ADVOCATES FOR HONEST AND DARING CREATIVE BUSINESS IDEAS."

—Raphaël De Andréis, President and CEO, BETC Euro RSCG

"The young generation of today is the smartest group of consumers that ever lived. They are informed, connected, and cynical. Only brands that are totally honest and transparent can aspire to win their hearts and minds. Brands will need to interact with this consumer all the time and provide an experience and a relationship that will connect them emotionally and rationally to their favorite brands."

—Douglas Patricio, Managing Director, Euro RSCG Latin America

"Digital youth understand what you're doing as they know the technology better. So they're both and biggest danger if you don't get it right."

"Today's youth are more cynical and more discriminating, but also more experimental and highly promiscuous when it comes to brands. Innovation, relentless new product development, experiential marketing, and relationship-building through PR and CRM are the real foundations we need to succeed with these digitally savvy, short-attention-span young customers. And that's not going to change much as they get older."

—Graham Lancaster, Chairman, Euro RSCG PR U.K.

"There is no doubt that today's younger consumers are discerning, creative, and knowledgeable, and this is coupled with an 'always on' multichannel existence that makes them more difficult to reach. But they, too, look for brands to offer them a competitive and relevant truth—brands that enable them, in a sociological sense, to define their social makeup. This fundamental human truth remains consistent, through time and across continents."

—Russ Lidstone, CEO, Euro RSCG London

marketers, and
your biggest potential

—Anthony Gregorio, CEO, Euro RSCG Group Australia

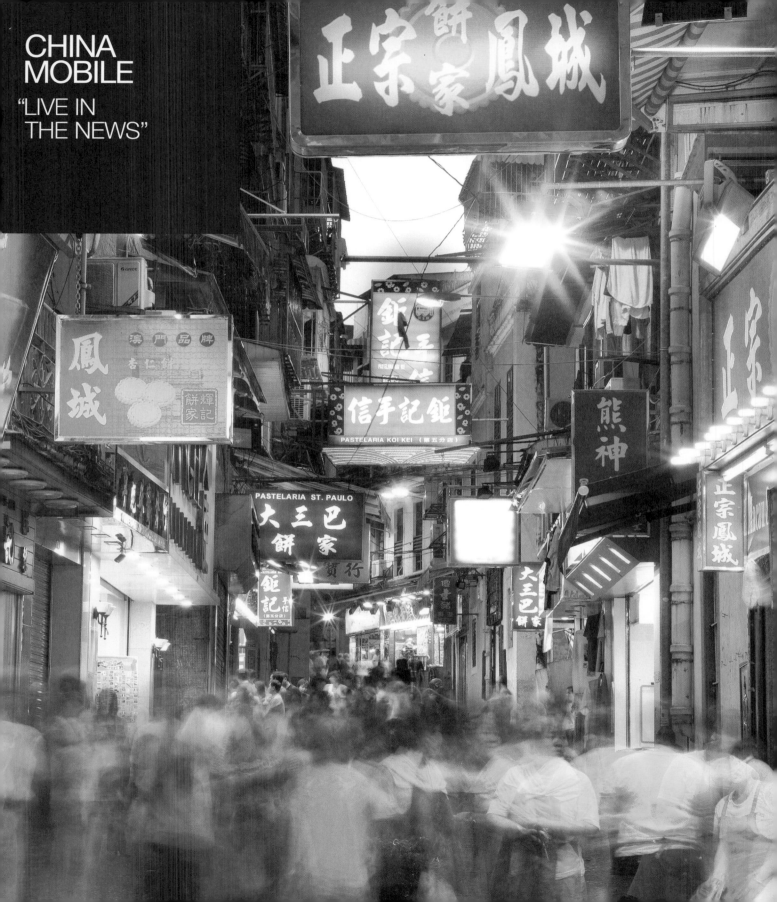

HOW DO YOU STAND OUT IN THE WORLD'S MOST CROWDED MARKET?

805 million. That's how many mobile-phone subscribers there were in China in 2010, making it the world's biggest market. The number one telecom in that market? China Mobile. But as recently as 2004, China Mobile's position wasn't so secure. That year, the Ministry of Information counted just 320 million mobile subscribers, and telecom companies nationwide were slashing prices to gain market share. The state-run company simply couldn't compete, and Euro RSCG had to find a way to lift it above the fray.

CREATING A UNIQUE NEW CELLPHONE SERVICE TO SET CHINA MOBILE APART

Guangzhou, a manufacturing hub in southeastern China, was a particularly competitive market. Automotive and biochemical jobs were luring people there every day, and the mobile-phone market was growing fast. These people were young, upwardly mobile, and interested in learning and experiencing new things. But how best to reach them? And, if China Mobile couldn't win on price, how could it compete with other telecoms?

The agency team needed to identify a point of differentiation for China Mobile that no other company could match. It started the creative process by examining the findings of Euro RSCG's 2004 Prosumer Pulse® study, a major ten-country survey. The report acknowledged China's fast-developing economic and technological clout but stressed that as China began to "catch up" to the West, its culture and history would continue to set it apart. "[A] distinctively Chinese characteristic and cultural strength over the years has been respect for learning," the researchers noted. "And despite the seduction of growing prosperity and glittering consumer goods, the Chinese still regard learning as a top priority." Seventy percent of the Chinese surveyed by Euro RSCG said lifelong education is the "best investment

a person can make," and 76 percent indicated that the news mattered more to them than it did five years prior. Among Prosumers, those figures rose to 80 percent and 84 percent, respectively.

With those insights in mind, the Euro RSCG team in Guangzhou spotted an opportunity to create an added-value service that would increase China

Mobile's brand value and raise revenue. Targeting early adopters, the agency conceived of an unprec- edented mobile news service that would keep up-and-coming Chinese professionals on top of all the latest news and events—quite a boost in a rapidly modernizing nation in which knowledge truly is power. "Live in the News" became China's first mobile data service, delivering daily news reports via SMS directly to users' mobile phones. Updates were delivered morning, noon, and night.

The next hurdle for the team was figuring out a way to make a big splash for the new service without

like newsprint would march through the city two by two, mingling with consumers and piquing interest in the new offering.

Government bureaucrats had concerns about the guerrilla campaign—young people parading through the city with messages affixed to their bodies smacked of a protest. Euro RSCG Guangzhou spent two months assuring officials at various levels that the newsprint would contain nothing more provocative than promotions for the new mobile service.

Once permits were in place, the human DM campaign took to the streets. The young models mingled with shoppers and businesspeople, handing out leaflets and chatting about the service. Commuters could hardly help reading about the service—the agency wrapped a subway car entirely in ads.

The effort earned China Mobile 328,000 subscribers to the news service the first month alone and a 68 percent boost in subscriptions overall. In the following month, 1.2 million additional subscribers signed on. Beyond new subscribers,

overrunning the client's limited budget. The shop's "Live in the News" campaign took a quite literal turn when creative executives hatched a plan to promote the new service via human "direct mail." Twenty-person teams of models wearing suits made to look the data service created an entirely new revenue stream for China Mobile. So successful was the Creative Business Idea that the telecom launched three more channels carrying shopping, nightlife, and real estate news and promotions later that year.

THE AGENCY TEAM WORKED TO ALLAY GOVERNMENT CONCERNS ABOUT PUBLICIZING THE NEW SERVICE THROUGH HUMAN "DIRECT MAIL."

[PROSUMERISM AMPED UP]

BY THEIR VERY NATURE, Prosumers are social and vocal. They have a lot to say, typically on a broad array of topics, and their opinions carry weight. That was our assumption in 2001 when we began formalizing our approach to them, and it was confirmed by our subsequent global studies. What we couldn't anticipate back then was how rapidly social media would develop and spread, and the galvanizing effect that would have on Prosumerism. Now we take it for granted that hundreds of millions of people around the world are plugged in to social media for hours every day, communicating things both profound and utterly inane. Back when we first identified Prosumers, online interactions were far more limited. Sure, Prosumers were quick to share their opinions on sites such as Amazon, Tripadvisor, and Epinions, but their reach extended only as far as the people who visited those particular message boards.

Then came the next generation of sites, where the interaction between users wasn't a by-product or sideshow but the main event. MySpace, Facebook, Twitter, and other

SoMe platforms put Prosumers on steroids, allowing them to do what comes naturally to them—communicating and sharing information—but on a far grander scale.

A SECOND ACCELERANT of Prosumerism has been the move of virtually everything online. Those of us who put together the initial Prosumer benchmark study would have been hard pressed to envision the extent to which—and the rapidity with which—the online and offline worlds would converge. Today, as we all are aware, virtually any product or service available in the brick-and-mortar world is available in the digital world as well—and often in superior form. This has given Prosumers the freedom to move seamlessly from one world to the next, taking a photo of something they're experiencing on the street, for instance, and transmitting it via e-mail, a social networking site, Flickr, or YouTube. There is no lag time now between "see" and "share." People no longer have to wait to run into someone they know or head home to pick up the phone to spread the latest word. It's input in, input out—all in an instant. And that has freed up Prosumers to engage in far more conversations than would have been possible a decade ago.

A THIRD PHENOMENON we have noted is the spread of the Prosumer mind-set. Some people are natural Prosumers, thanks to their innate curiosity, sociability, and drive. But now even mainstream consumers who don't share these traits are being infused with Prosumerist tendencies, thanks to the ease with which everyone can access and share information. This means we are seeing larger numbers of people exhibiting Prosumer behaviors such as comparison shopping online and expressing opinions in public forums. Even the slightest Prosumer tendency is facilitated and encouraged, making Prosumerism a self-reinforcing loop: The more people display Prosumer behavior, the more normal it becomes, and the more other people are apt to adopt it. Where's the risk when everyone else is doing it?

FOR MARKETERS, the speed and omnipresence of the new social technologies offer enormous opportunity, shortening the lag time between Prosumer and mainstream pickup of products and trends, and quickening the rate at which buzz zips across the world.

COMPELLING CHANGE

THE COMMUNICATIONS INDUSTRY rests on three skills: We share information and knowledge. We engage people. And we persuade people—to buy and do and even to think in a certain way. On behalf of clients, we apply these skills to motivate others to respond in a specific fashion, whether that means reaching for a particular brand of milk at the grocery store, taking out a certain car model for a test drive, or joining in some activity or movement. In other words, we influence attitudes and change behaviors.

So what if we were to set our minds to selling something other than milk and automobiles? What if we were to join together to help solve some of the world's greatest challenges—from AIDS to the clean water crisis to human rights abuses? There is certainly precedent for this: During World War II, in the United States, the War Advertising Council (WAC) was mobilized to support the Allied effort. Rosie the Riveter? Check. "Loose lips sink ships"? Also by WAC. In the ensuing years, the organization, now called simply the Ad Council, has gone on to create pro bono campaigns in support of such causes as protecting the environment (remember the "crying Indian" asking us to Keep America Beautiful?), the United Negro College Fund ("A mind is a terrible thing to waste"), and combating drunk driving ("Friends don't let friends drive drunk").

In some ways, the current work of the Ad Council and other pro bono efforts by ad agencies around the world can be likened to old-style corporate philanthropy, in which charitable efforts largely were one-off and relatively random—a financial contribution here, goods or services donated there. Corporate social responsibility (CSR) was business and industry's way of giving back and, perhaps more to the point, of getting credit for good deeds—creating a bank of goodwill that could be drawn upon in less rosy times. Just as people today are seeking to be more responsible and more conscious of how their consumption choices are affecting others and the planet we share, so, too, are companies moving in this more mindful direction. CSR—once an adjunct of business relegated to annual reports and press releases—has become central to the day-to-day workings and long-term strategies of a growing number of businesses. From GE and Google to Target and TOMS Shoes, companies are discovering that principles and purpose are not the enemies of profit.

The growing consumer mindfulness also means people are paying more attention to the companies with which they do business. Nearly three-quarters of Prosumer respondents (74 percent) to Euro RSCG's Future of the Corporate Brand survey (France, United Kingdom, United States) said they had become more interested in corporations' conduct and brand image over the past few years, and six in ten had actively looked for information on the reputation or ethics of a company in recent months. Perhaps most surprising, around half of Prosumers (49 percent) said that, with regard to advertising, they were more interested in learning about the company's values than about the product being sold. Following up on those findings, Euro RSCG's New Consumer survey discovered that people are paying more attention to the alignment of their own values and the values of their brand partners: Six in ten Prosumers say it is more important to them today to feel good about the companies with which they do business, and seven in ten prefer to buy from companies that share their personal values.

It's the job of marketers to help clients most effectively communicate their brand values and socially responsible behaviors, so that consumers may gain a more complete understanding of the people and purpose behind the brand. More personally, we believe that it's also the responsibility of our industry to use our communications skills to contribute to the common good, compelling people through our work to move in positive directions. Working together in a highly focused way, there's no question but that we have the power to bring about meaningful change.

In this chapter, we explore a number of agency cases focused on change, including efforts to reduce cigarette smoking and disease, influence a political movement, brighten up neglected communities, and harness the power of consumers around the globe to combat climate change and contribute solutions to some of the world's most pressing problems.

CAN A GLOBAL BRAND BRIGHTEN THE FUTURE?

When Euro RSCG London won Dulux's global account, the paint company asked for nothing less than global domination by 2014. It aimed to be the number one paint brand in every market, from the do-it-yourself-crazed shores of the United Kingdom to burgeoning middle-class homeowners in China. "Global domination" doesn't sound particularly friendly, but for Dulux conquering the world also meant changing it for the better.

The mission: add color to people's lives

MOST PAINT BRANDS MARKET their products as part of a weekend redecoration project, using glamour shots of color swatches and paint rollers in glossy magazines. To move Dulux to the top of the market worldwide, the agency had to think bigger than a wall, a window, or a door. Way bigger. "If you stop thinking about it as paint and start thinking about it as color, then it becomes about spiritual renewal and the benefit color can bring," says Russ Lidstone, CEO of Euro RSCG London.

That insight inspired the agency's Creative Business Idea: Dulux would become a global brand by using color to transform people's lives. Already committed to adding color to people's homes, the company would extend that pledge out into the world. The "Let's Color" campaign invited communities around the globe to participate in public painting projects aimed at lifting spirits, reinvigorating neighborhoods, and making the world a more pleasing place in which to live.

In March 2010, for instance, five classes of seven-year-olds at London's Virginia Primary School were handed rollers, brushes, and 1,140 liters of paint, all with their teachers' blessings. Euro RSCG London unleashed the children—with staff, parents, and other volunteers—on the bleak gray schoolyard, which was soon awash in a mix of sunny yellows, oranges, and reds.

The school chums weren't alone. In Jodhpur, India, residents paint their houses bright blue and dress in fiery shades as a way to cope with the surrounding desert landscape. "Everything is brown," says Kundan Singh, a spice trader interviewed for one of the Dulux documentaries shot by Euro RSCG London. "Vegetation burns. It's all the same view wherever you go, so wherever possible we paint." Dulux invited residents, business owners, and schoolchildren to come together to reinvigorate a drab square with 2,200 liters of blue and purple paint, a palette in line with Jodhpur's reputation as the "Blue City."

The "Let's Color" campaign has also refreshed cityscapes in Paris, Rio de Janeiro, Johannesburg, Istanbul, and elsewhere. "Every business has to ask itself, 'What is my social role?'" says Louis

Willem "Tex" Gunning, global CEO of AkzoNobel Decorative Paints. "Color has a tremendous impact on people's environments—and that means it can have an impact on their lives."

But the campaign isn't just a way to do good. "We want you to color your home, not just your schools or community centers," says Fernanda Romano, Euro RSCG's global creative director for digital and experiential. "It's really about the ultimate conversion: By seeing the psychological impact of color on neighborhoods, you are able to understand how it can also be used to improve life in the home."

The agency augmented the campaign with print advertising showing the transformation of interiors: a bare wooden staircase becomes a "red carpet,"

a garage is converted into a purple-walled home cinema, a bland rocking chair morphs into a vision in orange, all with the tagline "Let's Color."

The companion microsite integrates photos of Dulux's community events with more consumer-focused projects. A professional blogger posts entries about color, design, and public painting projects by the company and others. The site also offers consumers an opportunity to volunteer for future projects as well as links to the campaign's Twitter and Facebook accounts. "We want people to participate," Romano says.

From the start, enthusiasm for the project was contagious. At the scene of the Parisian paint event—an outdoor staircase at a public housing project—volunteers asked for more paint so they could continue the job on the building's other side. Online, blogs inspired volunteers to join the work crews. And just four months into the campaign, "Let's Color" had been featured on more than 700 independent blogs, including National Geographic's "Intelligent Travel," which called it "both worldly and beautiful." *The Walls* brand film was viewed 694,000 times and was voted Film of the Week on YouTube U.K.

"The films, the sociological implications, the social media—all are evidence of a modern brand in action," says Lidstone. The company announced plans to document as many as 500 painting events by 2015, each of which will communicate Dulux's place in the world and the power of its product. Says Gunning: "People will buy our brand because of what we do."

A MODERN BRAND IN ACTION

South Africa

Turkey

U.K.

India

Brazil

France

Orkut, Twitter, Flickr,
and Facebook were part
of the social media presence.
Content was "seeded" to
key bloggers worldwide.

- "THE WALLS" BRAND FILM WAS
  VIEWED 694,000 TIMES

- VOTED FILM OF THE WEEK
  ON YOUTUBE U.K.

- 12TH MOST TWEETED FILM

- 700 INDEPENDENT BLOGS

- THOUSANDS OF VOLUNTEERS

INPES
"ANTI-SMOKING
CAMPAIGN"

CAN PANIC BE GOOD FOR YOU?

When the French National Health Education Institute (INPES) asked BETC Euro RSCG in Paris to create an anti-smoking campaign, France's tobacco consumption was among the highest in Europe. In 2002, one in three men, one in five women, and nearly half of all teenagers smoked cigarettes. Each year 60,000 people died of cancer, costing the country more than €12 billion annually.

Until 2008, when the government banned smoking in restaurants, there were no taboos against public smoking anywhere in France. Far from considering cigarettes an imminent health risk, the French looked upon them primarily as a natural product derived from the tobacco leaf. And on smoking them as an inalienable French birthright.

The challenge was to reduce the number of happy smokers— those who were not interested in quitting.

For France's community of "happy smokers"—mostly teens to thirty-somethings—a future that included emphysema and cancer was too distant to matter. For them, smoking was glamorous, slimming, and, well, French.

Whereas prior campaigns had focused on offering advice and support to smokers who had already decided to quit, INPES and BETC Euro RSCG knew that targeting dedicated smokers—those who had no interest in quitting—was the key to driving down France's infamous smoking rate.

Happy smokers defied Euro RSCG's model for Prosumerism. In every other category, consumers were hip to marketing tactics and relentless product research. Cigarette smokers were another matter. They were willfully blind to the dangers of their own habit, sometimes wearing their ignorance as a badge of merit. They needed some cold water to wake up their inner Prosumer and douse their taste for tobacco.

Inspired by consumer reactions to reports about mad cow disease and genetically modified crops, Euro RSCG created a *War of the Worlds*–style report that would air during France's national news hour.

On Sunday, June 23, 2002, at 8 p.m.—traditionally a television hour for French families—the agency made its move with a 30-second ad consisting of a simple message on a black screen that told people a "consumption product" had been found to contain traces of cyanide, mercury, acetone, and ammonia. Viewers were urged to call the listed telephone number to find out more.

Within minutes, nearly 500,000 viewers lit up the phones. By the end of the evening, that number had doubled. The response so overwhelmed the system that only 10 percent of callers were able to get through to a recorded message informing them that the "consumption product" was cigarettes. For tens of thousands of others, the busy signals transformed worry into panic, sending unsuccessful

callers straight to the newspaper the next day. Even journalists were caught unaware, despite a press release sent the previous day. The overnight buzz became front-page news. An anti-smoking campaign had finally broken through in France.

Polling suggested the spot hit a nerve. Ninety percent of smokers surveyed said they believed the message, and 63 percent felt concerned by it. Half said the message "made them think." In the weeks following the TV ad, traffic to the quit-smoking hotline increased tenfold, and 20,000 people visited the INPES website. In the following 12 months, cigarette sales dipped 6 percent, the biggest drop since tobacco advertising had been banned in France a quarter century earlier.

Des traces de MERCURE, d'AMMONIAC,
d'ACIDE CYANHYDRIQUE et d'ACETONE
ont été décelées dans un produit
de consommation courante.

Pour plus d'informations appelez
gratuitement le 0800 404 404.

[Traces of mercury, ammonia, cyanide, and
acetone have been detected in a consumer product.
For more information call toll free 0800 404 404.]

ON SOCIAL RESPONSIBILITY

"AS ADVERTISERS AND MARKETERS, WE HAVE A GREAT RESPONSIBILITY TO PROMOTE SOCIAL CHANGE. IT IS COMMUNICATIONS THAT HELPS BRANDS SURMOUNT PRECONCEIVED NOTIONS AND ALLOWS CHANGE TO OCCUR. WE HAVE THE OBLIGATION TO IMPACT OUR CLIENTS' STRATEGIES AND DO THE BEST BY OUR SOCIETY."

—Laurent Habib, Managing Director, Havas in France and President, Euro RSCG C&O

"It's not enough to do good, you've got to let the world know what you're doing and why."

—Kate Robertson, U.K. Group Chairman, Euro RSCG Worldwide

"The era of blind consumption is over. Brands need to position themselves as agents for good that work toward positive change. Whether it be how a company treats its employees, its contribution to society, or its commitments and vision for the future, businesses will need to represent something meaningful to justify customer loyalty and premium prices."

—Agathe Bousquet, Managing Director, Euro RSCG C&O

"We tend to talk about corporate social responsibility and social media as though they are two separate entities. They are actually interlinked. The most socially responsible companies will derive huge benefits from social media, as their Prosumer fans act as powerful brand advocates."

—Marian Salzman, CEO, Euro RSCG Worldwide PR, North America

"Young people are savvy, passionate consumers, plugged into brands and trends and expecting business to contribute to the greater good. The challenge for brands is determining how to empower millennials and tap into their desire for positive change. We must engage them over the long term in a meaningful way."

—Olivier Pluquet, Havas Worldwide

THE SUN
"EU
REFERENDUM"

HOW DO YOU MAKE THE FRONT PAGE?

Gordon Brown may never have heard the old newspaper adage, "Don't argue with the man who buys ink by the barrel." But to be fair to the former prime minister, *The Sun* had brought its fight to him. Great Britain's most famous tabloid wanted to reestablish its political clout—and bolster its circulation—and Brown made the perfect mark.

THE Sun

Monday, September 24, 2007   20p   thesun.co.uk

EUROPE. NEVER HAVE SO FEW DECIDED SO MUCH FOR SO MANY

THE Sun SAYS

BRITAIN'S destiny is at stake today.

Gordon Brown is about to sign an EU Constitution that would change for ever the way we are governed.

Brown promised us a referendum in his campaign to become PM. Now he's giving two fingers to Britain.

In 1940 Winston Churchill said of the Battle Of Britain: "Never was so much owed by so many to so few."

Today The Sun launches a battle to win a referendum on the Constitution.

And we echo Churchill by declaring: Never have so few decided so much for so many. See Pages 2-7.

AN EU REFERENDUM. HE PROMISED IT, WE WANT IT

THE FIRST-EVER AGENCY-CREATED FRONT PAGE FOR THE SUN

On June 27, 2007, following the resignation of Tony Blair, Chancellor of the Exchequer Gordon Brown became the unopposed leader of the Labour Party and was invited by Queen Elizabeth to be prime minister. Brown inherited one of the most successful Labour administrations in party history, but Britons were uneasy due to wars in Iraq and Afghanistan and a new European Union constitution that would broaden Continental influence. Brown promised to hold a referendum on the latter, but later reneged.

The Sun has had a history of influencing the U.K. political landscape and championing the views of its readers. In 1992, the paper was so convinced of its contribution to the Conservative victory that it declared on the front page "IT'S THE SUN WOT WON IT." After years of Labour Party dominance in the U.K., the then editor of The Sun, Rebekah Wade, had a desire to reaffirm the paper's political impact, power, and persuasion. The challenge was to highlight The Sun's political clout, specifically by reminding Britain of the promise that Gordon Brown made to give the U.K. public a referendum on Europe. The best way to provoke the biggest reaction on the issue: target Prime Minister Brown directly.

The campaign broke on September 24, on the first day of the Labour Party Conference, the party's most important annual meeting. The tactic was irreverent and churlish, in perfect concert with The Sun's distinctive tone. Euro RSCG London developed an arresting visual for the campaign. They co-opted a famous wartime photo of Winston Churchill outside 10 Downing Street in which he flashed reporters the "victory" gesture, two fingers extended in a "V." The agency then superimposed Brown's head onto this iconic image of Churchill and pictured him giving two fingers to Britain. The new image broadcast the prime minister's inability to fill Churchill's massive shoes and at the same time implied Brown's hostile attitude toward the public. Accompanying copy bastardized one of Churchill's most famous quotes as "Europe. Never have so few decided so much for so many."

"This is typical Sun," says Naomi Troni, global chief marketing officer of Euro RSCG Worldwide. "To be provocative is in their DNA. It's totally spot-on. Still it took the paper to a new level, positioning them as a major player in the constitutional debate."

The image ran on the paper's hallowed front page, the first time an ad agency's artwork had ever appeared there. "Those covers are sacrosanct," says Roland Agambar, former marketing director of News Group Newspapers. "They're what sell the paper." That front page kick-started the tabloid's broader campaign for a constitutional referendum, which included extensive editorial coverage both in the paper and online. Alongside the editorials, the Brown/Churchill picture was featured on billboards and was even projected onto the Houses of Parliament, a 25-meter-high spectacle.

An ambient campaign was launched—centered on the seaside town of Bournemouth where the Labour Party Conference was being held and where, Troni explains, "there would be maximum embarrassment for Brown." A dozen men dressed in dark suits and wearing paper masks of Brown's face paraded around the town, riding a double-decker bus wrapped in the ads and reclining on the beach. Taxi receipts printed with the ads targeted other party members as they traveled to and from the conference.

The stunt ruined Labour's big bash and garnered attention from competing media, including BBC, Sky News, and Radio 4's *Today*. More than 100,000 *Sun* readers signed an online petition for the referendum within the first week of the campaign, and circulation figures topped 3 million.

Ultimately, *The Sun*'s readers didn't get their referendum. But they did get the attention of the prime minister: After just one day, Brown requested a meeting with editor Wade, asking her what he could do to get off the front page. The campaign ran for a week, a lifetime in the newspaper game. And when it came time to pick sides for the next election, *The Sun* backed Conservative David Cameron, declaring that "Labour's Lost It."

The outdoor and ambient campaign included projecting the signature image onto the Houses of Parliament.

SWISS
FEDERAL OFFICE
OF PUBLIC HEALTH

"LOVE LIFE.
STOP AIDS"

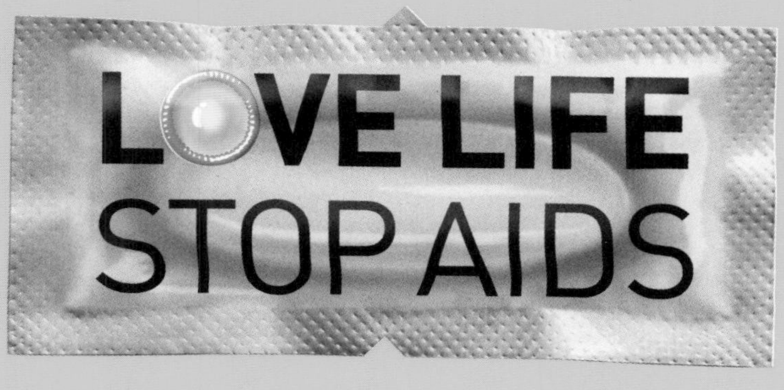

HOW DO YOU PUT THE BRAKES ON A QUICKIE?

In 2008, after decades of declining HIV rates, Switzerland posted a 20 percent spike in infections. Particularly affected: heterosexual men aged 36 and older. It was a development that puzzled everyone. Previous campaigns had depicted the fight against AIDS in a forceful and combative way, including one ad in which a boxer throws punches at the camera. They were powerful, so why were they no longer getting the message across?

"No one could explain it," says Peter Schaefer, Zurich-based planning director for Euro RSCG. The agency team's research to determine why so many people were letting their guard down uncovered the fact that new infections were largely a consequence of unplanned sex. "Unsafe sex almost invariably happens in the same situation: You need a condom, but you don't have one," Schaefer explains. "Travelers and businesspeople on holiday were particularly susceptible. You're under the influence of alcohol or you're traveling alone, and you make a choice that you wouldn't have made under normal circumstances."

Having identified the culprit, the agency launched a campaign to highlight the dangers of spontaneous sex. And how better to do that than by creating the quickest TV ads ever produced? Lasting just five to seven seconds each, the spots showed various couples exchanging a few words before getting down to business, along with the tagline, "Too quick to think of condoms?"

Funny ads underscored a serious problem.

The ads—strangers meet on a train/beach/tennis court, hook up on the sofa/bed/against the wall— were as much a product of budget as they were of strategy. As public awareness of HIV and AIDS had risen, the Swiss Federal Office of Public Health's budget had declined. The new super-short TV ads delivered impact on the cheap, while outdoor postings did the same.

Both forms of advertising drove nearly 40,000 people to the campaign website, where users could determine their risk factor. A pink background and playful interface put visitors at ease as they answered questions about their sex lives, most important of which was whether they had had unprotected sex. An encouragingly high 65 percent of visitors completed the assessment, and those judged to be at high risk were strongly advised to be tested for HIV. The site even provided a listing of local doctors. "It did everything but make the appointment for them," Schaefer says.

Event advertising continued the cheeky tone. At one sports festival, swimmers in condom-shaped swim caps raced across the lake to see who was "quickest." In cities, legions of bike deliverymen hired by the agency offered to deliver condoms just about anywhere. The service was tagged "We come before you come." The agency also distributed condoms with catchy slogans—"Quickie: 3 minutes. Putting on a condom: 10 seconds"— along with a multilingual flier containing safer-sex guidelines for natives and visitors alike.

Almost two-thirds of those exposed to the Love Life campaign remembered it. Most important, safer-sex habits rose 40 percent, and almost 20 percent of those who completed the survey and were identified as being at high risk underwent HIV testing and counseling. Meanwhile, widespread publicity and the targeting of travelers helped carry the "Love Life. Stop AIDS" message beyond Switzerland and into other markets.

[00:01] secs

**Too quick
to think of condoms?**

[00:03] secs

[00:04] secs

www.check-your-lovelife.ch

[00:05] secs

WORLD'S SHORTEST TELEVISION COMMERCIALS

STRANGERS MEET. STRANGERS HAVE SEX.

[00:01] secs

Too quick
to think of condoms?

[00:03] secs

LOVE LIFE
STOP AIDS

[00:04] secs

www.check-your-lovelife.ch

[00:05] secs

QUICKIE:
3 MINUTES

PUTTING ON
A CONDOM:
10 SECONDS

FREE CONDOMS SPORTED THE VITAL STATISTICS.

GIVING PEOPLE A ROLE TO PLAY

{

There's no shortage of opportunities for companies looking to engage consumers in their corporate social responsibility activities—and no dearth of rewards for doing so. By involving customers and other stakeholders in their good works, companies do more than create goodwill: They form deeper connections and open up new platforms of communication. A few lessons learned from brands that have done it well:

GIVE PEOPLE A SAY. Where decisions regarding corporate donations used to be made in private, now companies are recognizing the benefits of allowing consumers to direct their dollars. The American Express Members Project and Pepsi Refresh both allow participants to nominate worthy charities and vote on which will receive portions of millions of dollars in funding. This puts consumers in charge, making them feel more invested in both the cause and the brand. Multiple rounds of voting spanning several weeks or months amplify the effect.

MAKE IT REAL. Clicking on a link in support of a cause may be the extent of some people's desire to contribute, but others want to get a little skin in the game. "Give a Day, Get a Disney Day" was a hugely successful promotion created by Disney World. One million people volunteered a day of service to their communities through nonprofit organization HandsOn Network and were rewarded for that effort with a free one-day pass to a Disney theme park. Another great concept comes from Bolder (actbolder.com), an organization that connects socially minded companies with like-minded consumers. Businesses post challenges on the site and then reward individuals with discounts or free merchandise for completing them. The challenges range from the incredibly simple (turn off the tap while brushing your teeth, give someone a high five for a job well

done) to those that are somewhat more time- and labor-intensive (pick up litter around your neighborhood, bike to work). The payoff for the companies comes from attracting new customers, interacting with them on the site, and bonding over shared values.

MAKE IT EASY TO SPREAD THE WORD. Granted, this advice is pretty standard in the age of social media. People don't just want to do good; they typically want others to see them doing good and even join them in the effort. Pepsi Refresh does this particularly well. Each time a participant votes on an idea, he or she receives a word of encouragement (e.g., Yeah baby! or Good choice!) and is then asked to help promote the idea through links to Facebook, Twitter, and other social networking sites. With each project ranked by number of votes already garnered, it's easy to get competitive and be motivated to actively recruit others to vote for the "right" cause.

HOW DO YOU GET MILLIONS OF PEOPLE TO URGE WORLD LEADERS TO ACT TOGETHER?

With the 2009 United Nations Framework Convention on Climate Change (UNFCCC) in Copenhagen fast approaching, dozens of environmental groups were determined to make their voices heard but lacked focus and therefore critical mass. Former U.N. Secretary-General Kofi Annan asked Havas Global CEO David Jones to create a campaign to communicate not only the urgent necessity for action on climate change but also that time was running out for world leaders to commit to and attend the summit.

"Clearly, Mr. Annan's
of governments

TAKE A
STAND

BEDS ARE
BURNING

HOW CA
WE DAN
WHEN O
IS TURN

bility to convene and to unify really high profile leaders NGOs, and business was a unique opportunity."

—David Jones, Global CEO, Havas and Euro RSCG Worldwide

There was no money for the campaign.
The agency was working pro bono, but there would be limited media support if space had to be begged. There would be no high-cost television commercials running in prime time, no eye-catching ads in glossy magazines. The "Time for Climate Justice" campaign would have to circumnavigate the globe without a media budget. David Jones came up with two solutions: Firstly, the team would create the first-ever open-source campaign. They would put all the creative assets, including the logo, in the public domain so that anyone and everyone could, and would, use them, adapt them, own them. Secondly, they would ask advertisers and all their ad agencies to incorporate the visual assets into their own messages in their own paid-for space. With everyone being able to campaign and support the cause in whatever way they saw fit, the usual barriers to use and ownership were removed.

In developing the open-source assets, Euro RSCG couldn't chance the message getting lost in the cacophony leading up to Copenhagen; the agency had to come up with an idea that would amplify its campaign above all the rest.

"We needed a rallying cry," says Gerry Moira, chairman and director of creativity, Euro RSCG

London. The line the team devised was deceptively simple: "TckTckTck"—in other words, time is running out. The universal sound of a clock spelled out in text ensured universal understanding.

The accompanying logo—text on a field shaped like a dog tag—was designed to look unlike any other logo. Organizations could integrate it on posters and T-shirts without confusion. All campaign elements were available for download at timeforclimatejustice.org, including digital logo files, sound files of a ticking clock, and photos of global figures who were participating in the campaign such as Bob Geldof, Desmond Tutu, Jet Li, and Al Gore and celebrity campaigners such as Oscar-winner Marion Cotillard, pop singer Lily Allen, soccer star Clarence Seedorf of A. C. Milan, and tennis ace Yannick Noah.

Midnight Oil ceded rights to their worldwide hit "Beds Are Burning" and rewrote it to reflect the perils of climate change. The track was then rerecorded with a host of recording artists from around the world and produced by Euro RSCG's music label, THE:HOURS. Each download of the song counted as a digital signature to the online petition calling for an accord on climate change.

"To make a difference there had to be one

The open-source strategy worked. The song was downloaded a million times. Supporters bought more than 50,000 dog tags. Individuals and organizations worldwide began to riff on the campaign: Oxfam created a "TckTckTck" spot featuring actor Gael García Bernal. Actor Jet Li recorded a personal appeal and posted it on YouTube. At the 56th annual Cannes Advertising Festival, Euro RSCG encouraged other ad agencies to adopt the campaign; first up were Y&R, producing a spot in Brazil, and McCann Erickson, highlighting the campaign on their blog. "A lot of the strength of a creative idea is how shareable it is," Moira says. "It used to be that creative people were exceptionally possessive of their ideas. There was kind of a policeman role between the client and agency. The growing trend now is to create something and let it go."

In May 2009, the Global Campaign for Climate Action (a coalition of the largest NGOs) adopted "TckTckTck" as their global campaign. On December 8, 2009, supporters delivered a petition with more than 15 million signatures to Yvo De Boer, chief executive of the UNFCCC in Copenhagen.

Ultimately, the conference was a disappointment. No meaningful accord was struck. Still, Moira calls it "a glorious failure"—glorious because the campaign managed to unite an army of unaffiliated groups, deliver millions of signatures, and launch the world's first open-source campaign. And glorious, too, because the campaign's message—though not acted upon in Copenhagen—was heard by global leaders loud and clear. It was supported in an official U.K. government communiqué by then Minister for the Environment Ed Miliband, and, as it gathered pace, world leaders who had said they would not attend Copenhagen changed their plans one by one.

In 2010 the campaign lived on—once again serving as the unifying banner for the Global Campaign for Climate Action and the main campaign at Cancun.

message, and everyone had to own it."

David Jones, Global CEO, Havas and Euro RSCG Worldwide

**THE CAMPAIGN CREATED A
SINGLE VOICE BEHIND
KOFI ANNAN**

**A SONG THAT DELIVERED
A POTENT CALL FOR CHANGE**

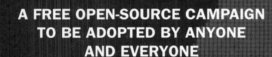

**"BEDS ARE BURNING"
DOWNLOADED
1 MILLION TIMES**

**A FREE OPEN-SOURCE CAMPAIGN
TO BE ADOPTED BY ANYONE
AND EVERYONE**

15 MILLION PEOPLE SIGNED THE PETITION WORLDWIDE

MORE THAN 120 CELEBRITIES PARTNERED IN THE EFFORT

"Decisions made by leaders are all short-term. If it's businesses, they make decisions for the quarterly results. If it's government leaders, they make decisions to stay in power. But the young look at problems from a completely different perspective; they have a long-term approach. All the existing problems are going to be theirs."

—Kate Robertson, Group Chairman, Euro RSCG U.K.

ONE YOUNG WORLD:

Tomorrow's Leaders Changing the World Today

92% OF GLOBAL RESPONDENTS TO EURO RSCG'S 2010 MILLENNIALS STUDY THINK THE WORLD NEEDS TO BE CHANGED

82% BELIEVE THEIR GENERATION HAS THE POWER TO BRING ABOUT THAT CHANGE

It's easy to talk in general terms about youth being "the future" or the "promise of tomorrow." David Jones, global CEO of Havas and Euro RSCG Worldwide, and Kate Robertson, U.K. group chairman of Euro RSCG Worldwide, decided that rather than just talk about it they would devise a creative strategy to activate that potential today. The result: One Young World (OYW), an annual global forum that organizes and empowers the next generation of leaders to shape a better future. Each year, hundreds of young people (born in 1985 or later) are nominated by leaders in business, government, and the nonprofit sector to attend a multiday summit in a world capital. Delegates are selected on the basis of their record of community involvement, commitment to solving global issues, and leadership skills.

IN FEBRUARY 2010, the OYW Inaugural Summit was held in London, bringing together nearly 850 of the best and brightest young leaders from 112 countries. At this first summit, the delegates focused on creating solutions in the six areas they identified as most vital: the environment, interfaith dialogue, the role of global business, developing global leadership, the media and its changing influence, and world health. The young delegates attended presentations and workshops on these topics led by highly esteemed and accomplished counselors from around the globe, including such luminaries as Nobel Peace Prize winners Desmond Tutu, Kofi Annan, and Muhammad Yunus, musician-activist Bob Geldof, and U.S. Senator John Kerry. Once back home, they began work on Ambassador Projects they had devised to address the six vital areas of impact. Babatunde Ogunlola, a delegate from Nigeria, for instance, has created One Young World Nigeria, the first program in that country dedicated to training high school prefects in leadership. In Venezuela, OYW delegates Jorge Isaac Casado and Jet Vargas work with nonprofit NGO Vitalis to promote environmental conservation and sustainable development through education. In the Philippines, Karl Molina is working to combat malnutrition among preschool students through education, supplementary medical and food-assistance services, and by promoting backyard and school gardens to increase household consumption of highly nutritious foods.

One Young World is but one example of how the Creative Business Idea principle and tools can be applied to larger causes. The global forum has already attracted the support of nearly 200 global brands, including Hewlett Packard, GE, Burt's Bees, Starbucks, and Nike. These companies sponsor delegates, paying for their travel and accommodations. The program offers yet another way for businesses to contribute to finding solutions to pressing local and global issues.

"Chemistry: the ability to work closely with complementary talent. Heart: often more important than talent is the heart of the creative, that drive that pushes him or her further than just talent. Courtesy: the ability to critique or share an opinion without ego or malice. All these… and a good night's rest."

—Rahul Sabnis, Executive Creative Director, Euro RSCG New York

"To feel free to say something silly. Great ideas often come from silly ones."

—Christophe Coffre, Vice President and Executive Creative Director, Euro RSCG C&O

"Extraordinary creative thinkers. It may seem like the obvious answer, but there can be no other. We can cover the walls with inspiring quotes and abstract images, but at the end of the day we either win or lose based on the brilliant minds we surround ourselves with."

—Kevin Pereira, Executive Creative Director, Euro RSCG Singapore

"A DESK, A CHAIR, AND AN OPEN MIND."

—Steve Coll, Executive Creative Director, Euro RSCG Australia

"Fun. Craziness. In other words: organized chaos."

—Neeraj Sabharwal, Creative Director, Euro RSCG Dubai

"The ability to have a laugh at it all every now and again…including yourself."

—Michael Lee, Executive Creative Director, Euro RSCG New York

"BEYOND THE PHYSICAL ENVIRONMENT, THERE IS THE SOCIAL ENVIRONMENT, AND MOST OF THE TIME THIS IS MORE IMPORTANT THAN A BEAUTIFUL CHAIR OR A POOL TABLE. THERE IS NO POINT IN HAVING THE BEST AND MOST MODERN FURNITURE IF TEAMS DO NOT INTERACT WITH EACH OTHER AND THERE IS NO CHEMISTRY WITHIN THE DEPARTMENT."

—Mariano Duhalde, Executive Creative Director, Euro RSCG Spain

"Passion, freedom, knowledge, fun, culture, personality, charisma, awards, innovation, daring, surprise, keep trying."

—Karim Achy, Creative Director, Euro RSCG Beirut

"TEAMWORK. SHARING OF IDEAS."

—Lee Garfinkel, Co-Chairman, Euro RSCG New York and Chief Creative Officer, Global Brands, Euro RSCG Worldwide

"Three Fs:

FUN—fun people, fun environment.

FAME—work being recognized, internally and externally.

FORTUNE—not being underpaid."

—CC Tang, Chairman, Euro RSCG Hong Kong and Chief Creative Officer, Euro RSCG Greater China

AS AN AGENCY CREATIVE MY SECRET WEAPON IS ...

"Stunning, sensational, inspirational, encompassing, elegant... design."

—Michael Lee, Executive Creative Director, Euro RSCG New York

"FEAR OF FAILURE."

—Gerry Moira, Chairman and Director of Creativity, Euro RSCG London

"KNOWING THAT MONEY HAS NO IDEAS. ONLY IDEAS MAKE MONEY."

—Jacques Seguela, Executive Vice President and Chief Creative Officer, Havas

"THE CALM BEFORE THE STORM."

—Rémi Babinet, Founder, BETC Paris and Global Creative Director, Euro RSCG Worldwide

"THE TRASH CAN."

—Frank Bodin, Chairman and CEO, Euro RSCG Group Switzerland

"My ability to surprise."

—Jonathan Deeb, Executive Creative Director, Euro RSCG South Africa

"Listening."

—Steve Coll, Executive Creative Director, Euro RSCG Australia

"Never stop trying to make the idea better."

—Lee Garfinkel, Co-Chairman, Euro RSCG New York and Chief Creative Officer, Global Brands, Euro RSCG Worldwide

"MY CLIENT. IF I'M TO BE THE BULLET, HE IS THE GUN. A GOOD CREATIVE NEEDS A CLIENT WHO CAN APPRECIATE, ENDORSE, AND COMMISSION."

—Elie Khairallah, Creative Director, Euro RSCG Arabia in KSA

"Being a grown-up who pretends to be a kid who pretends to be a grown-up."

—Christophe Coffre, Vice President and Executive Creative Director, Euro RSCG C&O

"Never being afraid to be an iconoclast at the beginning of every new project."

—Marcelo Bresciani, Creative Director, Euro RSCG Brazil

"My wife. She's a harsh critic."

—Mick Mahoney, Executive Creative Director, Euro RSCG London

"Courage."

—Stéphane Xiberras, Co-President and Executive Creative Director, BETC Euro RSCG

CREDITS

Polaroid
Pages: 18–25
Campaign: "Ambush"
Photography: Page 20, Nicholas Monu, Photodisc/Getty Images; Page 23, amana images inc./Alamy; Page 25, Digital Vision, Photodisc/Getty Images

Volvo
Pages: 30–37
Campaign: "The Mystery of Dalarö"
Actor: Anna-Lena Dahlberg
Actor: Goran Dahlberg
Actor: Lena Forssander
Actor: Peter Grip
Actor: Anders Holmquist
Photography: Pages 32–33, Frank Gross, Botanica/Getty Images

Evian, Danone
Pages: 38–45
Campaign: Film – "Roller Babies"
Country and Year: France, 2009
Actor/Model: Mathys Michotte c/o Ministar, Brussels, Belgium
Actor/Model: Lisa Yurtsever c/o Ministar, Brussels, Belgium
Actor/Model: William Duquenoy c/o Ministar, Brussels, Belgium
Production: Partizan
Music: Remixes of "Good Time"/ "Rapper's Delight"
Composers: Bernard Edwards, Nile Rodgers
Under editors: SONY/ATV, WARNER
Interpreted by Dan Nakamura aka "Dan The Automator"

Campaign: Film – "Waterboy"
Country and Year: France, 2003
Illustrator: So & Sau (Sophie Deiss & Jean-Christophe Saurel)
Music: "We Will Rock You"
Writer/Composer: Brian May
EMI Music Publishing France/Universal Music/Capitaine Plouf

Mortein
Pages: 50–53
Campaign: "Modern-day Ramayana"
Photography: Pages 50–51, Christopher Pillitz, Dorling Kindersley/Getty Images

Dos Equis, Heineken USA Inc
Pages: 54–61
Campaign: "The Most Interesting Man in the World"
Country and Year: USA, 2007–present
Actor: Jonathan Goldsmith – Most Interesting Man in the World
Actor: Claudio Marangone – Young Most Interesting Man in the World
Photographer: Michael Lewis
Photographer: Roger Snider

Select Comfort
Pages: 70–75
Campaign: "Sleep Number®"
Country: USA
Photographer: Jack Louth
Model: Brad Swanson
Model: Mellissa Brasier

Lacoste
Pages: 76–83
Campaign: Print – "KINGSTON: FW08"
Country and Year: France, 2008
Photographer: Phyl Pointer
Model: Vlada Rosyakova c/o Women
Model: George Alan c/o DNA
Model: James Neate c/o DNA
Model: Masha Tyela c/o Women
Model: Mathias Lauridsen c/o Ford
Model: Owen Stewart c/o Wilhelmina
Model: Gabriella Calthorpe c/o Women
Model: Mina Cvetkovic c/o Women

Campaign: Print – "MASTER SS10"
Country and Year: France, 2010
Photographer: Ellen Von Unwerth
Model: Lasse Pederson c/o Ford
Model: Lais c/o Women
Model: Mina Cvetkovic c/o Women
Model: Heloïse Guérin c/o Women
Model: Taylor Fuchs c/o Success

Billiken
Pages: 86–89
Campaign: "Billiken Club"
Photography: Page 86, White Packert, The Image Bank/Getty Images

Etoile
Pages: 92–95
Campaign: "Inside Magazine"
Photography: Pages 92–93, Digital Vision, Photodisc/Getty Images

Peugeot, PSA Peugeot Citroën
Pages: 96–101
Campaign: Film – "Motion and Emotion"
Country and Year: France, 2010
Production Company: Partizan Midi Minuit
Director: Michael Gracey
Director of Photography: Damien Morisot
Music: "Tonight"
Editors: All you need songs/Savoir Faire
Producers: Has been/Barclay/Universal
Composer: P.A. Busson
Sound Production: BETC Music
Music Supervisors: Christophe Caurret & Fabrice Brovelli

The All India Gems & Jewellery Trade Federation
Pages: 102–107
Campaign: "Lucky Lakshmi"
Photography: Pages 102–103, Art Directors & TRIP/Alamy

eBay
Pages: 108–113
Campaign: Print – "Ad Auction"
Campaign: "Table Football"
Country and Year: France, 2007
Featured Person/Model: Olivier Apers
Featured Person/Model: Cybel Villemagne
Featured Person/Model: Olivier Lancelin
Featured Person/Model: Flavio Fossati
Featured Person/Model: Bérénice Marlohe

Campaign: Print – "Ad Auction"
Campaign: "King and Princess"
Country and Year: France, 2007
Featured Person/Model: Léa Turbot
Featured Person/Model: Sébastien Turbot

Campaign: Print – "Ad Auction"
Campaign: "Garden"
Country and Year: France, 2007
Featured Person/Model: Aurélien Pecot

Air France
Pages: 130–135
Campaign: Print – "The Best Place on Earth, A Man Lying in the Grass"
Country and Year: France, 2006
Photographer: Jonathan De Villiers
Model: Luis Hernandez c/o Cap Prod Afrika

Campaign: Film – "The Best Place on Earth, The Swimming Pool"
Country and Year: France, 2006
Director: Hsien Hou Hsiao
Production: Première Heure/Radical Media
Model: Denni Nicola Parkinson c/o Zero Models
Model: Donovan Truter c/o Zero Models
Music: "Between the Miles"
Editors: Tactik Music + Clément Vaché + Leo Hellden
Authors/Composers: Daniela d'Ambrosio & Leo Hellden
Interpretation: Aswefall
Music Production: Kill the DJ Records

Campaign: Print – "The Best Place on Earth, A Woman Lying by a Tree"
Country and Year: France, 2006
Photographer: Horst Diek Gerdes c/o D & V Limited
Model: Silvia Ranguelova c/o Elite Model Management, Barcelona

Campaign: Print – "The Best Place on Earth, The Sun King"
Country and Year: France, 2006
Photographer: Stefan Ruiz
Model: Stephen Diehl c/o Irene Marie Management Group

Dr Scholl's, Merck Consumer Care
Pages: 136–139
Campaign: "Are you gellin'?®"
Country: USA
Actor: Bret Anthony
Actor: Ted Mattison
Actor: Buckley Sampson
Actor: Brady Smith
Actor: Chris Williams

The British Army, Army Recruiting Group
Pages: 140–147
Campaign: "Army on Everest"
Country and Year: U.K., 2006
Photography credit: Images courtesy of *Soldier* magazine

Jaguar
Pages: 152–161
Campaign: "Gorgeous"
Country and Year: Global, 2005–2007
Photographer: Michel Comte
Photographer: John Higginson
Model: Gelati Jorge Luis

RATP
Pages: 172–175
Campaign: Print – "Mobility"
Country and Year: France, 2001
Images courtesy of RATP

The Atlantic
Pages: 198–207
Campaign: Print – *The Atlantic, Think. Again"*
Country and Year: USA, 2008
Photographer: Christian Weber

McDonald's
Pages: 214–219
Campaign: Print – "Come as You Are, Woman"
Country and Year: France, 2008
Photographer: Richard Burbridge c/o Art and Commerce New York
Model: Theo/Femme c/o Jennifer Starr, New York

Campaign: Film – "Come as You Are, Dancer"
Country and Year: France, 2008
Model: Yannick Douzouo c/o DI, Paris, France
Production: Partizan
Director: Les Elvis

Campaign: Print – "Come as You Are, Gorilla"
Country and Year: France, 2009
Photographer: Vincent Dixon (Ask My Agent)
Actor/Model: Rosemary Bertilla (METROPOLITAN)

China Mobile
Pages: 222–227
Campaign: "Live in the News"
Photography: Page 222, JoSon, Stone+/Getty Images

INPES
Pages: 246–251
Campaign: "Anti-smoking Campaign"
Photography: Page 246, Ryuichi Sato, amana images/Getty Images; Page 248, Ken Anderson, Photodisc/Getty Images

The Sun, News Group Newspapers
Pages: 254–261
Campaign: "EU Referendum"
Country and Year: U.K., 2007
Photography: Houses of Parliament Projection
Photographer: Andrew Stczynski

Global Humanitarian Forum, Time for Climate Justice
Pages: 270–277
Campaign: "TckTckTck"
Country and Year: Global, 2009
Photographer: Robert van Waarden
Additional photography: Images courtesy of Greenpeace; Pages 274–275, Paul Taylor, Digital Vision/Getty Images

ACKNOWLEDGMENTS

First and foremost, thank you to the core team, without whom this book would not have been possible: Patrick Armitage, Ann O'Reilly, and Naomi Troni.

We are also grateful for the contributions of a wider group of people whose efforts and determination have made it all happen: Angie Argabrite, Ellen Broome, Julia Gates, Joe Guyt, Marian Salzman, Nancy Wynne, and Deanna Zammit.

Thanks to all of the Euro RSCG people, past and present, from around the network who provided their thoughts, help, enthusiasm, and encouragement in the making of this book:

Moshe Abehsera, Euro RSCG New York
Matt Atkinson, Euro RSCG 4D
Sicco Beerda, Euro RSCG Netherlands
Cristina Bergamo, BETC Euro RSCG
Ryan Berger, Euro RSCG New York
Ann Bradford-Griffith, Euro RSCG C&O
Philippe Brandt, BETC Euro RSCG
Seb Buckley, Euro RSCG London
Brune Buonomano, Euro RSCG C&O
Coleen Cahill, Euro RSCG New York
Amy Cartwright, Euro RSCG Australia
Georgia Caumon, BETC Euro RSCG
Anne-Isabelle Cerles, BETC Euro RSCG
Frederique Corcia, BETC Euro RSCG
Fanny Dalmau, THE:HOURS
Leslie Dubest, THE:HOURS
Marielle Durandet, BETC Euro RSCG
Mercedes Erra, Euro RSCG Worldwide
Michael Fanuele, Euro RSCG New York
Aicha Fetouhi, BETC Euro RSCG
Rori Floyd, Euro RSCG New York
Daniel Floyed, Euro RSCG Worldwide

Stéphane Fouks, Euro RSCG Worldwide
George Gallate, Euro RSCG 4D
Mali Ganly, Euro RSCG Buenos Aires
Ana Garcia Salinas, Euro RSCG Buenos Aires
William Gibb, Euro RSCG Luxe
Jake Goodman, Euro RSCG London
Camille Guillotin, BETC Euro RSCG
Jun Hagiwara, Euro RSCG New York
Tasha Hanna, Euro RSCG New York
Marleen Haverkamp, Euro RSCG 4D Amsterdam
Don Hogle, Euro RSCG New York
Héloïse Hooton, BETC Euro RSCG
Marianne Hurstel, BETC Euro RSCG
Martha Kenny, Euro RSCG 4D Amsterdam
Makram Khater, Euro RSCG Dubai
Andrew Knox, Euro RSCG Australia
Shelby Kovant, Euro RSCG New York
Clarisse Lacarrau, BETC Euro RSCG
Michelle Lai, Euro RSCG China
Emma Langford-Lee, EHS 4D
Benjamin Lazarus, Euro RSCG San Francisco
Christine Leblond, BETC Euro RSCG
Andrea Lee, Euro RSCG Singapore
Eugénie Lefebvre, BETC Euro RSCG
Russ Lidstone, Euro RSCG London
Yvette Lim, Euro RSCG Singapore
Claus Lindorff, BETC Euro RSCG
Brittany Lippett, Euro RSCG London
Gabrielle Low, Euro RSCG Worldwide
Jean-Baptiste Lucas, BETC Euro RSCG
Christine Maik, Euro RSCG Singapore
Muneni Matimba, Euro RSCG 4D Amsterdam
Tanya Merchant, Euro RSCG New York
Katy Milmoe, Euro RSCG New York
Gerry Moira, Euro RSCG London
Fabien Moreau, THE:HOURS

Ken Mulligan, Euro RSCG London
Jeanne Nicastro, Euro RSCG New York
Erminia Nusswitz, Euro RSCG C&O
Hilary Olesen, Euro RSCG New York
Jake Palmer, Euro RSCG London
Sushant Panda, Euro RSCG India
Daphne Pang, Euro RSCG Singapore
Mary Perhach, Euro RSCG New York
Kirk Peterson, Euro RSCG New York
Catherine Philippe, BETC Euro RSCG
Cathy Pitegoff, Euro RSCG New York
Maryann Pulvirenti, Euro RSCG New York
Kate Robertson, Euro RSCG Worldwide
Alexandre Rodionoff, BETC Euro RSCG
Fernanda Romano, Euro RSCG Worldwide
Julie Rosenoff, Euro RSCG New York
Rich Roth, Euro RSCG Tonic
Marc Saint-Ouen, Euro RSCG C&O
Alexandre Sap, THE:HOURS
Peter Schaefer, Euro RSCG Zürich
Lindsay Sherman, Euro RSCG New York
Sarah Shubrook, Euro RSCG Luxe
Phil Silvestri, Euro RSCG Tonic
Betsy Simons, Euro RSCG New York
Saloni Singh, Euro RSCG India
Carole Smila, Euro RSCG London
Suman Srivastava, Euro RSCG India
Andrew Stadelberger, Euro RSCG New York
Peter Sun, Euro RSCG Worldwide
Marty Susz, Euro RSCG Tonic
Michael Tam, Euro RSCG China
Jessica Tarpey, Euro RSCG London
Lara Thomas, Euro RSCG Luxe
Chris Thompson, Euro RSCG Tonic
Kate Todd, Euro RSCG London PR
Anna Toussaint, Euro RSCG C&O
Mical Valusek, Euro RSCG Buenos Aires
Melissa Vodegel Matzen, Euro RSCG KLP
Holly Ward, Euro RSCG London PR
Marianne Weinmann, Euro RSCG Zürich

Valerie Wernick, Euro RSCG Tonic
Yorko Yin, Euro RSCG Shanghai
Jihan Zakhem, Euro RSCG Dubai
Amanda Zalka, Euro RSCG New York

A special thanks to former Euro RSCG
Worldwide chairman and CEO Bob
Schmetterer, an early champion of the
agency's Creative Business Ideas platform
and the author of *Leap: A Revolution in
Creative Business Strategy* (Wiley, 2003),
one of the sources we turned to as we
reviewed details of select case studies.

And, of course, we are tremendously
grateful to all our clients who allowed us to
share their Creative Business Ideas—we
couldn't have done it without you.

And finally, our thanks to the whole team
at Smallwood & Stewart. It's been a
genuine pleasure working with you:
John Smallwood, Carol Bokuniewicz,
Tara Romeo, and Laurie Orseck.

Many thanks
to all our colleagues
and clients who
helped bring our
first decade of
Creative Business Ideas
to life.

Stay tuned for the
next generation!

ISBN: 978-0-917841-02-6

Printed in Thailand
10 9 8 7 6 5 4 3 2 1

Produced by Smallwood and Stewart,
5 East 20th Street, New York NY 10003

Design: Carol Bokuniewicz Design

If our ideas succeed,
our clients succeed,
and so we succeed.
It's as simple as that.